Verity Cole

2

IELTS Introduction

Study Skills

A self-study course for all Academic Modules

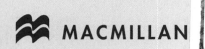
MACMILLAN

Macmillan Education
Between Towns Road, Oxford OX4 3PP
A division of Macmillan Publishers Limited

Companies and representatives throughout the world

ISBN 978-0-230-42573-6

Text, design and illustration © Macmillan Publishers
Limited 2012
Written by Verity Cole

First published 2012

Designed by eMC Design Ltd.
Illustrated by Oxford Designers & Illustrators Ltd pp 11, 12, 27,
46, 47, 48, 49, 65, 67, 70, 79
Cover photograph by Corbis/Oliver Rossi
Picture research by Catherine Dunn

Author's acknowledgements

Many thanks to Macmillan for giving me this opportunity.
Thanks above all to Susan Cole, my mum, for all her support
over the years – I could never have achieved what I have
without you.

The publishers would like to thank Sam McCarter.

The authors and publishers would like to thank the following
for permission to reproduce their photographs:

Bananastock p31; BrandX p68(tr); **Corbis**/Bettmann p34,
Corbis/Ocean p24; **Getty Images** p23, Getty Images/National
Geographic p68(b); **Image Source** p55; **Macmillan Australia**
p66; **Stockbyte** p15.

Graphs and Tables reproduced with the kind permission of:

HESA Student Record-Reproduced by permission of the Higher
Education Statistics Agency Limited, HESA cannot accept
responsibility for any conclusions or inferences derived from the
data by third parties p40; Internet Users-www.internetworldstats.
com p42(t); Office for National statistics pp42 fig 2, 39, 45, 46;
United States Bureau of Labour Statistics p41; www.Unicef.org
p42 fig 1; www.UIS.unesco.org p42 fig 3: World Trade
Organisation p44; World Tourism Organisation p72.

The author and publishers are grateful for permission to
reprint the following copyright material:

Page 23: Material adapted from 'Chats, flirting and travel
rows - Jumbo is just like us' by Cal Flyn, copyright © News
International Syndication Ltd, first published in *The Sunday
Times* 05/06/2011, reprinted by permission of the publisher;

Page 24: Lumir G. Janku for an extract and figure adapted
from 'Ancient Flying Machines' by Lumir G. Janku,
www.world-mysteries.com, copyright © Lumir G. Janku;

Pages 30–31: The Hershey Company for an extract adapted
from "The History of Chocolate" www.allchocolate.com.
Reproduced with permission of The Hershey Company;

Page 34: Nick Taylor for an extract adapted from "The Great
Depression" by Nick Taylor, *New York Times*, copyright ©
Nick Taylor;

Page 36: Jacobs School of Engineering, University of
California, San Diego for an extract adapted from "Coming
to TV screens of the future: A sense of smell", University of
California, 15 June 2011, as published on *ScienceDaily*
http://www.sciencedaily.com;

Pages 45–46: Office for National Statistics for the charts
and table "Percentages of works by home-to-work travel
time"; "Duration of commute from home to work by region
of workplace" and "Median hourly earnings by travel time,
London and Rest of the UK" October-December 2009,
United Kingdom, from *Commuting to work*, 02/06/2011,
www.nomisweb.co.uk , © Crown copyright;

Page 66: Material adapted from "Telescope to detect ET on his
mobile' by Jonathan Leake, copyright © News International
Syndication Ltd, first published in *The Sunday Times*
03/07/2011, reprinted by permission of the publisher;

Page 68: National Geographic Society for an extract adapted
from 'The Real Price of Gold' by Brook Larmer, *National
Geographic*, January 2009, http://ngm.nationalgeographic.com,
copyright © National Geographic Society.

Printed and bound in Thailand

2016 2015 2014 2013 2012
10 9 8 7 6 5 4 3 2 1

Contents

Welcome to *IELTS Introduction Study Skills*. This is a different kind of exam practice book. As well as providing you with exam practice materials, this book will:

Familiarize you with the different question types you will find in IELTS and give you guided practice in each of them.

Help you to develop the skills you need to be successful.

There are four parts, corresponding to the four IELTS modules. Each part begins with *skills development*. In these sections you will develop your skills through focused exercises, with detailed guidance given in the key to each question. Next, in the *skills practice* sections, you can put what you have learnt into practice. Finally, the book contains a complete *Practice test*.

As *IELTS Introduction* is aimed at students starting at around band 3–4, some of the reading and listening texts are shorter or the questions are a little easier than you would find in IELTS, especially towards the beginning. Essential vocabulary is given in a glossary. This will support you as you gradually develop your skills and improve your IELTS score.

For Writing and Speaking both model answers and sample student answers are given, so that you can start to evaluate your own work. Useful language is also provided.

The book is intended to be used for self study, but could also form the basis of a short intensive IELTS preparation course.

The IELTS Exam

IELTS, or the International English Language Testing System, is an exam designed to assess your level of English, on a scale from 1–9. The score you need will depend upon the course and the university you want to study at, but many students find they need to get an overall band score of 6.

Each section is weighted equally, but it is possible to get half band scores for the Reading and Listening modules (eg 5.5, or 6.5), but only whole number bands (eg 5, 6, 7 etc) for Speaking and Writing. Overall, therefore, you may get a half band score.

Band 9 – Expert User
Has fully operational command of the language: appropriate, accurate and fluent with complete understanding.

Band 8 – Very Good User
Has fully operational command of the language with only occasional unsystematic inaccuracies and inappropriacies. Misunderstandings may occur in unfamiliar situations. Handles complex detailed argumentation well.

Band 7 – Good User
Has operational command of the language, though with occasional inaccuracies, inappropriacies and misunderstandings in some situations. Generally handles complex language well and understands detailed reasoning.

Band 6 – Competent User
Has generally effective command of the language despite some inaccuracies, inappropriacies and misunderstandings. Can use and understand fairly complex language, particularly in familiar situations.

Band 5 – Modest User
Has partial command of the language, coping with overall meaning in most situations, though is likely to make many mistakes. Should be able to handle basic communication in own field.

Band 4 – Limited User
Basic competence is limited to familiar situations. Has frequent problems in understanding and expression. Is not able to use complex language.

Band 3 – Extremely Limited User
Conveys and understands only general meaning in very familiar situations. Frequent breakdowns in communication can occur.

Band 2 – Intermittent User
No real communication is possible except for the most basic information using isolated words or short formulae in familiar situations and to meet immediate needs. Has great difficulty in understanding spoken and written English.

Band 1 – Non User
Essentially has no ability to use the language beyond possibly a few isolated words.

Band 0 – Did not attempt the test
No assessable information provided.
A summary of each module is outlined below:

Listening

The Listening takes about 40 minutes and each section gets progressively more difficult.

Part	Number of speakers	Number of questions	Situation	Example
1	2	10	social/ general	conversation between a student and a landlord
2	1	10	social/ general	welcoming talk for a group of new students
3	2–4	10	academic	students in a seminar discussion
4	1	10	academic	a university lecture

Question Types: multiple choice, completing notes or sentences, completing or labelling diagrams, charts or tables, classifying, matching and writing short answers.

Exam Tips: You will only hear each section ONCE. However, there is time to look briefly at the questions before each part is played. During the exam, you should write on the question paper, and at the end you will have 10 minutes to transfer answers to the answer sheet. It is important to do this carefully, and check grammar and spelling, as mistakes will lose marks.

Academic Reading

The Reading lasts one hour and there are three reading texts, of increasing difficulty, taken from newspapers, magazines, books and journals. The topics are of general interest, so learners do not have to be experts in the subject area to understand them.

Question Types: multiple choice, choosing *True/False/Not Given*, or *Yes/No/Not Given*, identifying the view of the writer, completing sentences or notes, completing or labelling diagrams, charts or tables, classifying, matching, choosing paragraph headings and writing short answers. There are 40 questions in total.

Exam Tips: As with the listening module, answers are written on an answer sheet, but no extra time is given for this. It is important that you practise managing your time (20 minutes for each section) so that you can complete the whole module within the hour by reading quickly and efficiently.

Academic Writing

There are two tasks in this module and it lasts 1 hour.

Task	Time	Number of words	Description of task
1	20 minutes	At least 150 words	Describe, compare and contrast information in diagrams, charts or tables, *or* describe the stages of a process, *or* explain how something works
2	40 minutes	At least 250 words	Give solutions to a problem, *or* present arguments in favour and against an opinion, *or* give and justify an opinion.

Assessment: In order to do well in Task 1, it is important to answer the question clearly, and organize your answer well. This may include grouping data appropriately and describing trends, rather than detailing every piece of information given. Your answer also needs to be accurate and include a good range of vocabulary.

In Task 2 slightly different assessment criteria are used. Here you need to ensure that you answer the question and include a clear and logical argument, giving evidence or examples where appropriate. Your answer also needs to be well organized and have a variety of vocabulary and grammatical structures used accurately.

Exam Tips: It is important to keep to the timings, as Task 2 is longer, and carries slightly more weight than Task 1. It is also important to keep to the word limits, as writing less than the number of words stated is likely to result in a lower score.

Speaking

The Speaking module takes between 11 and 14 minutes and is an oral interview between the learner and an examiner. The interview will be recorded.

Part	Time	Description
1	4–5 minutes	General questions about home, family, studies, etc.
2	3–4 minutes	You are given a card with a topic and 3–4 prompt questions on it. You have 1 minute to prepare, and then have to speak for 1–2 minutes on that topic. At the end, the examiner may ask you a question.
3	4–5 minutes	Further discussion questions relating to the subject in Part 2. This section requires you to give opinions, speculate and express reasons.

Assessment: Assessment is based on your fluency, the range, and accuracy of the vocabulary and grammatical structures you use, and your pronunciation.

Exam Tips: Try to relax during the exam, and give more extended responses to questions rather than just 'yes' or 'no' to gain higher marks. You can prepare for this module, for example, by practising speaking for 1–2 minutes on different topics. However, don't memorize long speeches as examiners can usually spot this, and will ask you to talk about something else.

Study Skills: Listening

The Listening module is the first part of the IELTS exam. Do this quiz to see how much you know about it.

Quiz

1 The Listening test lasts for about .... minutes.
   A forty **B** eighty **C** twenty

2 There are forty questions and .... points.
   A eighty **B** forty **C** twenty

3 You will hear each part of the listening ....
   A twice **B** once **C** three times

4 You have some time to read the questions before the listening starts. True or false?

5 You have some time to transfer your answers onto the answer sheet when the listening finishes. True or false?

6 In the first section of the listening you hear
   A two people talking **B** one person talking
   C up to four people talking

7 In the second and fourth sections of the listening you usually hear
   A two people talking **B** one person talking
   C up to four people talking

8 In the third section of the listening you hear
   A two people talking **B** one person talking
   C up to four people talking

9 Choose **two** correct answers.
   Sections 3 and 4
   A are more difficult than Sections 1 and 2.
   B are easier than Sections 1 and 2.
   C have more academic content than Sections 1 and 2.
   D have more information about social situations than Sections 1 and 2.

10 You need to know a lot about academic subjects to do well in the exam. True or false?

Section 1

Skills development

Completing a form: predicting topic vocabulary

Listening module
Section 1:
Exam information
Number of people: two (a dialogue)
Context: conversation about a social situation
Example situation: a student applying for a bank account

Remember
Read the question carefully before you listen. Think about the meaning of each of the words on the form and the topic. Predict which words you will hear for each gap. This will help you to listen for *key* information (i.e. the most important information). For example:

Application to join the health centre
Previous doctor: ....
Medical history: ....

> Key words could be: *health, doctors, illness, medicine.*

> You will hear a name of a doctor here. You'll probably hear the title 'Doctor' (Dr) and then a surname.

> This is about past health problems so you'll hear descriptions of the person's past illnesses. You might hear some names you don't recognize, but the speaker will probably spell them

1 Look at the possible titles 1–3 below and read the form. Choose the best title for the form. Underline key words in the form which helped you choose the title.

   1 Bank account application
   2 Job application
   3 Accommodation form

Surname:	1 ....
Initials:	2 ....
Marital status:	3 ....
Occupation:	4 ....
No. of bedrooms:	5 ....
Preferred location:	6 ....

2 ⊙01 Complete the form using words from the box. Then listen to Part 1 of the conversation and check your answers.

single	student	three singles	city centre	C.J.	Minguez

Understanding letters and numbers

1 ⊙02 How do you say these letters in English? Write the letters in the correct group. Listen and check your answers.

A	B	F	G	H	L	O	P
Q	R	S	U	V	W	Y	Z

1 /eɪ/, as in p<u>ay</u>: J, K, ...
2 /iː/, as in b<u>ee</u>: C, D, E, T, ...
3 /e/, as in <u>e</u>gg: M, N, X, ...
4 /aɪ/, as in fl<u>y</u>: I ....
5 /əʊ/, as in n<u>o</u>: ....
6 /uː/, as in t<u>oo</u>: ....
7 /ɑː/, as in c<u>ar</u>: ....

Remember
- You can write numbers like this: *3*, or like this: *three*
- You can write dates like this: *October 9/ October 9th*, or this: *9 October / 9th October*
- You can use abbreviations if they are recognized around the world e.g. *the U.K.* (but not *Sat.* for *Saturday* or *Oct.* for *October*)

2 ⊙03 Listen to three similar answers **A–C** and number them in the order that you hear them.

1 A 07778 8976364	**B** 07788 8976364	**C** 0788 8976364
2 A £402	**B** £4,002	**C** £42
3 A August 10, 2013	**B** September 8, 2013	**C** September 18, 2013
4 A h_atkinson@twinky.it	**B** h.atkins-son@twinky.it	**C** ha@atkins_it

3 ⊙04 Now listen to Part 2 of the conversation between the student and accommodation officer and complete the form.

Monthly rent:	**7**	....
Starting:	**8**	....
Contact – phone:	**9**	....
email:	**10**	....

Avoiding mistakes

1 Read the exam question and look at the student's answers. Find three mistakes.

Questions 1–8

Complete the form below.

Write **NO MORE THAN TWO WORDS AND/OR A NUMBER** for each answer.

Remember
- Use the correct spelling or you will lose points.
- Follow the instructions in the exam question carefully; if it says 'no more than two words', don't write three.
- Words and numbers written with hyphens count as one word e.g. *thirty-three*
- Contractions count as two words e.g. *he's, I'd* etc.

Library card application form

Name: (1) *Robert Flack*

Gender: (2) *he's male*

Age: (3) *twenty-one*

Year of study: (4) *first yeer*

Hall of residence: (5) *John's College*

Subject: (6) *Engineering*

Type of degree: (7) *BA**

*Short for Bachelor of Arts, the type of qualification you get if you study a degree subject like English, History or Philosophy. If you study a science, your degree is BSc (Bachelor of Science).

Sentence completion: dealing with extra information

1 Match sentences **1–3** to extracts **A–C** below from the recording script. Underline information in **A–C** which is similar to information in **1–3**.

   A I've thought about the basketball club, but I'm not sure if I can go to all of the practice sessions. One of them, on a Wednesday evening, is at the same time as an evening lab lesson I have.

   B Yes, I know, but the problem is that I don't know which club to join and they all need us to enrol now – in the first week of term.

   C Yes, well that is a problem because one of the rules is that your attendance must be 75%. I suppose if you don't go to most of the sessions, it's a waste of money.

   1 Students have to enrol in clubs at the start of ....

   2 .... club is on a Wednesday evening. .....

   3 Students must go to .... % of the club sessions. .....

2 Complete each sentence **1–3** with one word from the recording extract.

3 ⊙ 05 Listen and complete sentences **4–8**.

   4 If students join more than one club, they get a .... % discount.

   5 Linda thinks aikido is a .... sport.

   6 Some of Aisha's .... begin at 9 a.m.

   7 Aisha is excited about joining the ....

   8 The students agree to go to ballroom ....

Skills practice

Now practise the skills you have learnt by answering questions **1** and **2**.

1 ⊙ 06 For questions **1** and **2**, listen and choose the correct answer, **A**, **B** or **C**.

   1 How many people will be going on the trip?

     A fifteen   **B** seventeen   **C** thirteen

   2 How old are the students?

     A over eighteen   **B** over nineteen   **C** over twenty

2 For questions **3–10**, complete the form and the tutor's notes below. Write **NO MORE THAN TWO WORDS AND/OR A NUMBER** for each answer.

Czech Tours Booking form	
Date of arrival	(3) ....
Date of departure	(4) ....
Type of accommodation:	Hostel
Length of stay (nights):	(5) ....

Prices of hostels: Charles Bridge Hostel is (6) .... Koruna / €30

Castle Hostel (7) £25 / € ....

Charles Bridge phone: (8) 00 420 ....

Castle Hostel email: (9) ....

Opening hours of Charles Bridge: (10) 9 to ....

Skills development

Listening module Section 2: Exam information
Number of people: one (a monologue)
Context: non-academic, social needs
Example situation: an informal talk on how to open a bank account

Completing a flow chart: listening for key words

1 Look at the title of the flow chart below. Do you think the speaker will describe:

   a different parts of an object?

   b different stages over time?

   c different points in an argument?

2 Look at the name of each phase and try to guess what it means. Then underline key words in each sentence in the flow chart.

3 07 Now listen and answer the questions.

   1 Do you hear the key words that you've underlined?

   2 Are the stages in the diagram in the same order as they are in the talk?

   3 Are the words in each sentence in exactly the same order as they are in the talk?

4 Now listen again and complete the sentences. Write one word for each answer.

The different phases of culture shock

Honeymoon phase
A (1) .... period which can last for over two weeks.

Culture shock
Feeling (2) .... or frustrated about living in a foreign country.

Coping
1 Teach people about your (3) .... and culture.
2 Buy ingredients from local shops and (4) .... your favourite meal.
3 (5) .... things you like about England.

Acceptance
Knowing what it is about life in the UK which makes you (6) ....

Remember
- Read the information in the flow chart and think about what you know about the subject.
- Listen for 'signposting' words and phrases, e.g. *The first phase ... second phase ... This is the final phase.* These will help you know when to move on to the next part of the flow chart.
- The order of the points in the listening is the same as the order of the questions.

Labelling a map: using visual clues

1 Look at the map of the town and read the directions. Choose the correct letter, **A**, **B** or **C**.

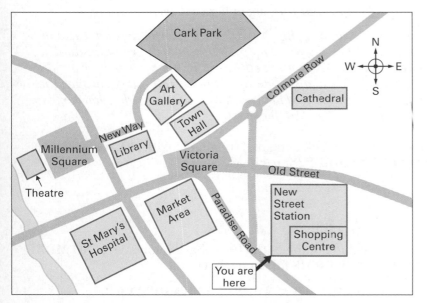

1 Go north, cross Old Street, turn right at the roundabout and continue down the road. What is on your right?
  A Colmore Row
  B the cathedral
  C the town hall

2 Go north-west, up Paradise Road, and cross Victoria Square. What is in front of you?
  A the library
  B the art gallery
  C the town hall

2 Answer the questions below.

1 What's between the library and the theatre?
2 What's next to the shopping centre?
3 What's north-east of the art gallery?
4 What's opposite the market area?

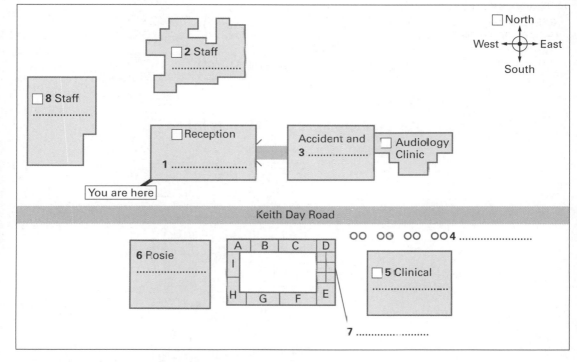

3 Look at the map above and answer the questions.

1 Where are the people in the listening on the map?
2 Find these things on the map: *doors, corridor, road.*
3 ⊙ 08 Listen and tick the words you hear on the map.

- There are two main types of map labelling task. In the first, you label a map with words, in the second you match letters on the map with labels.
- The speaker may use complex sentence structures, for instance, the passive verb form e.g. instead of *we are here, we are situated here*

4 ⊙**09** Listen and read the extract of the recording script below and underline the information for labels 1–3 on the map.

Good morning and welcome to your first day of your student placement at our wonderful hospital. I do hope that your time spent here will be interesting.

Right, well, as you'll already have seen, the hospital site is enormous, and it's quite easy to get lost, so I'll start by showing you a map. At the moment, you are situated here, just in front of the reception in the main entrance. To the north of here are the staff apartments, where you'll be staying while you work here. If you go through the double doors to the right of reception and head east along the corridor, you come to the Accident and Emergency ward or A&E for short.

5 ⊙**10** Now listen to the rest of the talk and label the map. Write **NO MORE THAN TWO WORDS AND/OR A NUMBER** for each answer.

Skills practice

Questions 1–4

⊙**11** Now listen to the recording and complete the flow chart below. Write **NO MORE THAN TWO WORDS AND/OR NUMBERS** for each answer.

New student mentor programme: order of events

> (1) .... the students to the Halls of Residence. Show them their rooms.

> Take students on tour of campus. Show them the facilities e.g.
> (2) ...., library, doctors etc.

> Bring students to collect their (3) ....

> Take students for dinner in the (4) ....

Questions 5–12

For questions **5–12** label the map below.

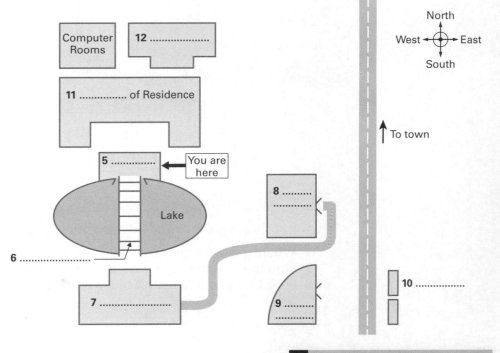

Skills development

Listening module Section 3: Exam information
Number of people: up to four people
Context: education or training
Example situations: a tutor and a student discussing an assignment, or a seminar situation with several students talking

Multiple choice: listening for synonyms and detail

Remember
Try not to choose an option just because you hear one word from it. Think about the whole meaning of what you hear.

1 ⊙**12** Read **1** and **2 A–C** and write synonyms for the underlined words. Then listen to the first part of the conversation and check your answers.

  1 Sue can't do her <u>assignment</u> because (synonym: e ....)
  A she doesn't think any of the subjects are <u>interesting</u>. (synonym: f ....)
  B she doesn't know which <u>subject</u> to write about. (synonym: t ....)
  C she didn't get good <u>grades</u> for any of her essays. (synonym: m ....)

  2 The lecturer suggests
  A Sue writes more about photography.
  B Sue gives a <u>talk</u> in the next seminar. (synonym: p ....)
  C Sue looks again at <u>20th-century</u> art. (synonym: m ....)

2 ⊙**12** Now listen again and choose the correct letter, **A**, **B** or **C** in **1** and **2**.

Short answers: listening for detail

1 ⊙**12** Listening for detail is important in short answer questions. Listen to the conversation again and match each number (**A–D**) to what it refers to.

  1 subjects studied in a term   **A** hundreds
  2 century   **B** nineteenth
  3 mark for photography essay   **C** sixty
  4 books on modern art   **D** nine

2 ⊙**13** Now listen to the second part of the conversation and answer the questions below. Write **NO MORE THAN ONE WORD OR A NUMBER** for each answer.

  1 What changed the paintings of artists like Claude Monet? ....

  2 How many female artists can Sue name? ....

Matching: identifying opinions

1 In matching tasks, it's useful to recognize different ways of expressing opinions. Complete the table with comments 1–5 from the recording script below.

Interested in the subject	Has doubts about the subject	Not interested in the subject

  1 I'd prefer not to write about the same paintings again.
  2 I'm sure you're right, but I'm having trouble thinking of ideas.
  3 I could try that I suppose, but it does sound quite difficult.
  4 Well, I might write about that, but I'm not sure it inspires me.
  5 I'll definitely research that further.

2 Read the pairs of sentences **A** and **B**. Choose the sentence which expresses the strongest opinion.

> **1 A** I could write about that.
>   **B** I'll definitely write about that.
> **2 A** I'd like to research that further.
>   **B** I might research that further.
> **3 A** You may like to consider modern art.
>   **B** You should consider modern art.

3 ⊙**13** Listen to the second part of the conversation again and write the correct letter **A**, **B** or **C**, next to topics **1–3**.

What does Sue decide about each of these subjects?

> **A** She wants to write about this.
> **B** She has doubts about this.
> **C** She doesn't want to write about this.

> **1** Impressionist paintings
> **2** Modern art
> **3** Contemporary art

Skills practice

Now read the exam questions below, then listen to the recording and answer the questions.

⊙**14** For questions **1** and **2**, choose the correct letter, **A**, **B** or **C**.

1 Claire has had problems because
   A her students misbehave.
   B she works too hard.
   C she's suffering from stress.

2 The tutor wants Josh to
   A take his students to an interesting lecture.
   B make friends with his students.
   C set work for students to do on their own.

For question **3**, choose **THREE** letters, **A–F**.

3 Both Claire and Josh
   A have taught teenagers.
   B talk too much.
   C need to read some books.
   D get on well with their students.
   E have difficulty getting their students interested.
   F have enjoyed their teaching experience.

⊙**15** For questions **4–6**, listen to the second part of the conversation and choose one adjective **A–E** for each person.

How does each person feel about next term?

> **A** hopeful
> **B** angry
> **C** disappointed
> **D** excited
> **E** worried

> **4** Josh
> **5** Claire
> **6** The tutor

Skills development

Listening module Section 4: Exam information
Number of people: one (a monologue)
Context: education or training
Example situations: a lecture. The subject may be quite specific, but remember that you do not need any specialist knowledge to answer the questions.

Recognizing paraphrasing

1 Read sentences **1–5**. Replace the underlined words with a word from the box.

unhealthy	work out	put on	disorders	overate

1 Young adult women <u>ate too much</u> ....

2 Mothers <u>gained</u> weight ....

3 Office workers didn't <u>exercise</u> ....

4 Teenagers have eating <u>problems</u> ....

5 Elderly people had a(n) <u>bad</u> diet ....

2 ◎**16** Listen to extracts from Part 1 of the listening and complete the sentences with key words.

1 *Good morning, everyone, and thank you all for coming to my talk. As you may know, as part of our training to become dieticians, we have to do some research into an aspect of dietary health. You've already heard talks from my classmates on diabetes and eating .... or 'eating ....' among teenage .... between 12 and 16 who are influenced by images in ....*

2 *My research falls into two parts. The first part consisted of primary research; I collected data by conducting a survey. About a fifth of the people questioned were .... with young .... They said that they had .... weight during pregnancy and then couldn't lose it again.*

3 *About one in ten people questioned weren't worried about their weight at all. These tended to be people .... the age of ....· Interestingly, these people were aware that ...., fatty food could lead to weight ....·*

4 *Around a quarter of people interviewed worked ten to twelve hours a day and typically, spent a lot of time .... in front of a ....· This group generally said that they ate healthily but didn't .... enough to burn the calories off.*

5 *Just over 30% of people thought they .... because of how they felt. This group tended to be .... in their ....*

Remember
There are usually one or two more options than you need in a matching task.
Before you listen, think of different ways of saying the options in the test.

3 ⊙17 Now listen to Part 1. Match the correct ending (**A–G**) to each sentence **1–5**.

1 Teenagers have eating problems ...
2 Mothers gained weight ...
3 Elderly people had a bad diet ...
4 Office workers didn't exercise ...
5 Young adult women ate too much ....

A because they thought it **improved life**.
B because they **worked long hours**.
C because they were **middle aged**.
D because of **issues in their lives**.
E because they didn't have **active lives**.
F because they **didn't have time to plan meals**.
G because of the **media**.

4 Read the recording script on page 92. Underline phrases which relate to the words in bold in **A–G**.

Completing a summary: recognizing differences in sentence structure

1 Match sentences **1–4** from the summary below to sentences **A–D** from the listening. Then underline the correct word in this sentence:

In summary completion tasks, the order of words in sentences on the question paper is usually *the same as/different to* the order of words in the listening.

Summary	Listening
1 How heavy you should be relates to your height.	A But why is obesity a growing problem? Well, researchers have found a number of explanations.
2 Obesity levels tend to be low in Asian countries (5%) and higher in Western countries (75%).	B When people reach the age of 50 and older, they tend to put on weight.
3 There are several reasons behind the increase in obesity.	C This is used to calculate your ideal weight on the basis of how tall you are.
4 The older you are, the more weight you gain.	D Levels of obesity are at 5% in China and Japan. In contrast, in England, Germany, and the USA, up to 75% of the population are obese.

2 ⊙18 Now listen to Part 2 and complete the summary. Choose one word from the box for each answer.

age   children   city   height   location   low   world

Researchers have used the Body Mass Index to measure levels of obesity around the (1) .... The BMI relates your weight to your (2) .... to calculate how heavy you should be. They found that obesity levels are (3) .... in Asia and higher in Western countries.

Levels of obesity in (4) .... are high in 79 developing countries. There are several reasons for the increase in obesity. One is to do with (5) .... Another reason relates to (6) .... If a person lives in a (7) .... they are less active and can become overweight.

Completing notes: predicting word class

Remember

In a note completion task, it is important to read the notes first before you listen. This will give you an idea of the subject or context of the talk. You may be able to predict some of the words you will hear. Look at the words that come before and after each gap. This will help you to understand the type of word which you will need.

1 Read the student's notes taken during a lecture and answer the questions.

    1 What subject do you think the lecture is on?

        A geography: the study of the earth and its features and of life on the earth

        B history: the study of past events, particularly in human affairs

        C palaeontology: the study of the forms of life existing in prehistoric or geologic times, as represented by the fossils of plants, animals, and other organisms

    2 What type of animal is *Samrukia nessovi?* How many other animals of the same type are mentioned in the notes?

2 Read the student's thoughts (**a–d**) and look at the notes below. Which answer (**1–10**) does each thought refer to?

a It's after an article (*a*) so I probably need a countable noun.

b It's after a modal verb (*could*), so I probably need another verb.

c It's after an adjective, so I probably need a noun.

d It's after a noun and before a preposition and another noun, so I probably need a verb.

Samrukia nessovi

Nature of discovery:	Two bones found in (1) ...., in Kazakhstan. Bones (2) .... to a large bird. Lived 100 (3) .... years ago – at the same time as dinosaurs.
Previous research:	Giant (4) .... and dinosaurs lived at different times. The only bird that lived then was the size of a (5) ....
Size of *Samrukia Nessovi*	(6) .... was approximately 30cm in length. Height of bird: more than (7) .... metres tall. Weight of bird: more than 50 kg – (8) .... than an ostrich.
Comparisons	• Elephant bird of Madagascar was (9) .... – 500kg. • Giant Moa of New Zealand was taller – 4 metres.
Questions	Unknown whether it could (10) ....

---

3 Think about the type of words you need for the other gaps.

4 ⊙**19** Now listen and complete the notes. Write **ONE WORD ONLY** for each answer **1–10**.

Recognizing topic sentences

Remember
Lecturers often introduce what they are going to say with a sentence which summarizes each part of the talk. These are called topic sentences. Try to listen out for these sentences as they will help you to find where you are in the notes.

1 ⊙19 Read the headings in bold in the notes on page 17. Put the topic sentences **A–E** in the correct order. Then listen and check your answers.

A So, how big was the bird?

B There are many questions surrounding the recent discovery.

C This doesn't, of course, make it the biggest bird ever to have lived on earth.

D Up to now, palaeontologists thought that dinosaurs and large birds did not live at the same time.

E Well, it's certainly an exciting time to be studying palaeontology at the moment.

Skills practice

Now read the exam questions below, then listen to the recording and answer the questions.

1 ⊙20 For questions **1–6**, listen and complete the notes. Write **ONE WORD ONLY** for each answer **1–6**.

```
                    Fashion Marketing

What does the (1) ...................... want?
• Durability - how (2) ...................... a product lasts.
• Style - Is the product (3) ......................?
• Comfort

(4) ...................... market:

Which group of people would buy a particular product?

Areas that fashion marketers work in:

(5) ..............................., product development, branding,
pricing, publicity, sales promotion,(6) ...............................
and forecasting
```

2 For questions **7–12**, complete the summary. Write **ONE WORD ONLY** for each answer **7–12**.

> Market researchers meet the (7) ...., conduct surveys and research competitors.
>
> Marketing (8) .... sell products to chains of stores. They consider whether their product goes with other items that the store (9) .... They also research the store's consumers.
>
> Fashion marketing isn't (10) .... because fashion marketers have a lot of power. Fashion marketing involves (11) .... work and tight deadlines. It's a good idea to get some unpaid work (12) .... because this will make you more attractive to future employees.

How much do you know about the IELTS Academic Reading module? Do the quiz below and find out.

Quiz

1 Complete the sentences with these words.

> one   three   forty   sixty

1 The Academic Reading module has .... reading passages.

2 There are .... questions in this module.

3 There is .... mark for each correct answer.

4 You get .... minutes to complete the reading test.

2 You have extra time to write your answers on the answer sheet at the end of the exam. True or false?

3 Reading passages sometimes have pictures or tables. True or false?

4 Choose the correct answer.

1 Each reading passage is
   A between 700 and 800 words long.
   B more than 1,000 words long.
   C between 400 and 500 words long.

2 Reading passages are from
   A books only   B books and magazines
   C books, magazines, journals and newspapers
   D books, magazines, journals, newspapers and letters

5 These are some of the common question types in an IELTS exam. Match the question types (A–F) to their descriptions (1–6).

A true, false, not given
B matching headings
C multiple choice
D matching sentence endings
E sentence / summary / note completion
F diagram completion

1 Read the passage and write labels on a picture.
2 Choose the correct ending for the beginning of a sentence.
3 Read the passage and fill in the missing information.
4 Decide if a statement agrees with the information in a passage.
5 Choose one or more answers from a number of different possible options.
6 Choose the correct heading for each section of the passage.

In this section, you will be looking at the skills you need to do well in the IELTS Academic Reading module and practising different question types.

Reading Passages 1, 2 and 3

Skills development

Getting a general understanding of the passage

1 Read the title of Reading Passage 1 and answer these questions.

Future of money: a currency that helps people make friends

1 Can you find another word for 'money' in the title?
2 Scan paragraphs A and B of the passage and find more words that relate to 'money'.
3 Scan paragraphs A and B of the passage again and find words that relate to 'technology'.

Remember
You need to get a general idea of what a passage is about. The title of the passage often contains its main ideas. You can also read through the passage quickly or 'scan' it, looking for words which relate to the main ideas.

Future of money: a currency that helps people make friends

New game with a social purpose

A In one of America's poorest cities, a new use of technology has been attracting attention. The 92,000 people who live in Macon, Georgia, USA know each other a little better than they did, thanks to an online computer game. Since October, the locals – college students and elderly people alike – have been playing Macon Money, a 'social impact game' that uses 'virtual money' to bring people from different economic backgrounds closer together by encouraging them to meet.

B In the game, winning players receive 'bonds', which they can then exchange for bank notes of Macon Money. These notes can be spent at local shops and businesses. But the game is not as simple as it sounds. Each person receives just half a bond and must find the person with the other half so that they can spend it. People often find their other half by searching for them on the social networking sites Facebook and Twitter. Matching players then meet in person to redeem the bond and get their Macon Money. The bonds range in value from $10 to $100.

C Pairs might spend their money separately, or do something together like share a meal or give the money to someone who needs it more, says Beverly Blake of the John S. and James L. Knight Foundation, the non-profit group based in Miami, Florida, that funded the game. 'These are meetings and conversations that might not happen naturally at all,' she said. The game's designers are hoping Macon Money will bring members of the community together who wouldn't normally meet each other.

D Although Macon Money is quite a new innovation, early signs are positive. The first round of the game has seen $65,000-worth of bonds given out and 2,688 participants so far spending $48,000 in Macon Money. Recently, Macon Money's Executive Producer Kati London accepted the 2011 FutureEverything Award for outstanding innovation in art, society and technology in Manchester, UK. It isn't just technology for technology's sake, London said in an interview with FutureEverything after receiving the award, 'It's about putting those tools, that craft, to work in the community.'

E Whether such a game can bring lasting economic growth remains to be seen, however. An independent research firm will now evaluate how much economic activity the game has caused, with results due later this year.

Remember
In the exam, there are often more headings than you need. Before you start doing the task, check how many paragraphs the passage has and how many headings you need. Read the headings before you read the passage to help you focus on the main ideas you need to look for. There is only one correct heading for each paragraph. Make sure that the heading you choose summarizes the whole paragraph.

Matching headings to paragraphs

1 How many paragraphs does the passage have? How many headings does it need?

2 Read the list of possible headings. Underline the most important words in each one.

> **List of headings**
>   **i** A game that makes money
>   **ii** Investigation of financial benefits
>   **iii** The creation of unusual partnerships
>   **iv** New game with a social purpose
>   **v** Success at an early stage of the project
>   **vi** The way the game works
>   **vii** Strategies for using social networking sites
>   **viii** Charities that benefit from the project
>   **ix** Success at a late stage of the project

3 Look at the extract from the text below. Which piece of underlined information in the paragraph tells us about the purpose of the game?

New game with a social purpose

A In one of America's poorest cities, ¹a new use of technology has been attracting attention. The 92,000 people who live in Macon, Georgia, USA know each other a little better than they did, thanks to an online computer game. Since October, the locals – college students and elderly people alike – have been playing Macon Money, a ²'social impact game' that uses 'virtual money' ³to bring people from different economic backgrounds closer together by encouraging them to meet.

4 Read paragraph **B** and find information which matches headings **vi** and **vii**. Which heading matches the paragraph? Why? Why is the other heading not correct?

5 Read paragraphs **C–E** and choose the correct heading for each one.

True, False or *Not Given*: understanding the difference

Tips for completing *True, False* or *Not Given* tasks

In these tasks, the statements will not be expressed in the same way as the relevant information in the reading passage.

Follow these steps to complete these tasks.

Read the statements and underline the most important words. Then find information in the reading passage that has a similar meaning. If you can do this, the answer to the statement is *True*.

If there isn't any information in the passage with a similar meaning to the words in the statement, look for information with the opposite meaning. If you find this, the answer is *False*.

The answer is *Not Given* if only some of the information in the statement is in the passage, but not all of it.

1 Look at the underlined information in statements **1–3** below. Then answer questions **A–D** using information from Reading Passage 1.

1 The money which people get from playing Macon Money <u>isn't real</u>.	**A** Which word in paragraph A means the same as 'not real'?
2 People can buy things in shops <u>all over the USA</u> with Macon money.	**B** What adjective in paragraph B describes the shops and businesses where you can spend Macon notes?
3 <u>More young people</u> play Macon Money online <u>than old people</u>.	**C** Can you find another way of describing old and young people in paragraph A? **D** Does the passage say how many old and young people play the game?

2 Do the statements **1–3** above agree with the information in the Reading Passage? Write:

TRUE	if the statement agrees with the information
FALSE	if the statement contradicts the information
NOT GIVEN	if there is no information on this

3 Now decide if these statements are *True*, *False* or *Not Given*.

1 A computer game has brought the people of Macon closer together than they were before.
2 Everyone who wins the game receives the same amount of money.
3 Most people decide to give their money away to poor people.
4 People from different areas of Georgia have met through Macon Money.
5 The game's inventor has become very rich with Macon Money.
6 All of the Macon Money bonds which have been given out have been spent.
7 More research is needed to see whether Macon Money has created a healthier economy.

Yes, No, Not Given questions: recognizing the claims of the writer

Remember
There are different types of *Yes, No, Not Given* questions in the exam. Sometimes the task will ask you if a set of statements reflects the claims of the writer and sometimes whether they reflect the writer's opinion.
An opinion is a personal feeling. Opinions often start with the words *I believe, I feel, I think, in my opinion, in my view*. Sometimes the writer uses adverbs to show their opinion, eg *luckily* – to say that he thinks something is lucky; *sadly* – to say he thinks something is sad.
A claim is a statement that a writer makes. The writer often uses evidence from scientific study to support their statement. A claim is not necessarily true.

1 Read the short texts **A–D**. Which are claims and which are opinions?

A Do animals have or feel emotion? I cannot tell you the number of times I have been asked that question. My answer without even looking for any specific emotional studies on animals is simply YES. Having lived with animals most of my life I feel very positive that every emotion that we feel is also felt by our pets.

B Charles Darwin's ideas about evolution argue that animals have emotions and know the difference between right and wrong.

C Unfortunately, some people are over sentimental about animals. They've grown up watching cartoon animals with human emotions and believe that real life animals are the same.

D According to researchers, cows enjoy mental challenges and feel excitement when they use their intellect to solve a problem. Dr Donald Broom, a professor at Cambridge University, says that when cows figure out a solution to a problem, 'The brainwaves showed their excitement; their heartbeat went up and some even jumped into the air. We called it their Eureka moment.'

2 Read the first paragraph of Reading Passage 2 and choose the best title **1–3**.

   1 Differences between elephants and humans revealed.
   2 Similarities between humans and monkeys revealed.
   3 Similarities between elephants and humans revealed.

3 These phrases are used to talk about research, and writers may use them to introduce claims. Scan the passage to find the words and phrases.

argues that	claims that	conclude that	demonstrates	describes
details evidence of	conclude that	reveals	proved that	found to be

4 Read the statements and answer questions **a–c**. Then decide whether the statements **1–3** reflect the claims of the writer in the reading passage. Write:

YES   if the statement reflects the claims of the writer
NO   if the statement contradicts the claims of the writer
NOT GIVEN   if it's impossible to way what the writer thinks about this

   1 Although we don't look like elephants, our brains work in a similar way.
     a Find a word which relates to 'look like' in paragraph A.
     b What do we do with our brains? Find a noun that relates to this in paragraph A.
     c Does paragraph A say that our brains work in a <u>similar</u> way to elephants'?

   2 This is the first study which demonstrates that elephants can feel emotions.
     a Find three words that relate to elephants' emotions in paragraph B.
     b Find a word in paragraph B which means 'to watch or study something'.
     c What has been shown for the first time: elephants' emotions or the different types of elephant emotions?

   3 Elephants communicate with each other using a range of sounds.
     a What does 'a range' refer to in paragraph B?
     b What do elephants use to greet one another and show they want to play?
     c Paragraph C refers to a 'conversation'. Does it say anything about the sounds elephants make?

A A 35-year study, in which approximately 2,500 elephants were observed in Kenya, has collected evidence of behaviour that claims that human beings have certain characteristics in common with elephants. Whereas our appearance is not unlike that of monkeys, the study argues that we definitely share similar emotional reactions and thought processes with elephants.

B Elephants' human-like behaviour, such as showing sadness when one of their family (or herd) dies, has been observed before. However, the study – the Amboseli elephant research project – reveals for the first time the range of emotions that elephants can show. For instance, the study demonstrates that elephants feel upset when another elephant is in pain, feel angry over disagreements and can recognize members of their family.

C The body language used by elephants is also recognizable to humans. The study describes elephants touching trunks or bumping shoulders in greeting, while 'playful' elephants moved their heads from side to side to start a game. In addition, the researchers thought they saw evidence of 'conversation' between the elephants; when the signal to move was given, elephants stood side by side and 'discussed' which route to take. When this long exchange ended, the elephants moved all together in one direction.

D The project also details evidence of elephants' higher thinking skills. When one of the herd was shot with a tranquilizer dart two elephants were observed removing the dart and standing either side of the tranquilized elephant in order to prevent it from falling over. Elephants also have the ability to make and use basic tools, such as fly killers taken from tree branches, and the knowledge to remember routes through the landscape many years after they last travelled them. They have been found to be more intelligent than apes in some areas, such as route planning, while other experiments have shown them as capable as monkeys in co-operating on tasks. Scientists have even proved that their short-term memories are better than humans' in some respects.

E Cynthia Moss started the Amboseli elephant research project. Her findings, published by University of Chicago Press conclude that there is 'no doubt' that elephants display empathy for one another. There is considerable support for her findings. Iain Douglas-Hamilton, who runs the Save the Elephants project in Samburu nature reserve in Kenya, welcomed Moss's research. 'They're definitely compassionate animals,' he said.

> **Glossary**
> observe – to watch or study someone or something with care and attention
> characteristic – a particular quality or feature that is typical of someone or something
> trunk – an elephant's long nose
> tranquilizer dart – a small pointed object with a drug on it that makes animals calmer when they are very worried or nervous
> ape – a type of animal without a tail that includes chimpanzees and gorillas
> empathy – the ability to understand how someone feels because you can imagine what it is like to be them

5 Do the following statements reflect the claims of the writer in the reading passage? Write:

YES   if the statement reflects the claims of the writer
NO   if the statement contradicts the claims of the writer
NOT GIVEN   if it's impossible to say what the writer thinks about this

1 Scientists have found that elephants can recognize and mirror human body language.
2 The study shows that elephants work together in order to make a decision.
3 The project demonstrates that some elephants have a good sense of direction.
4 The research has found that elephants are cleverer than humans and monkeys in some ways.
5 Moss's findings differ from the conclusions of all other scientists.

Now practise the skills you have learnt by answering the questions on the following reading passage.

Reading passage 3

The mysterious origins of flight

A Flight has been the dream of humankind since birds were seen in the sky. But it wasn't until the 1780s that two Frenchmen flew in a hot air balloon near Paris. After that, powered flight became the goal. Although it was thought that flight was possible as early as the 13th century, and in the 16th century Leonardo da Vinci drew designs which looked like aircraft, it wasn't until the Wright brothers made their first successful flights in *Kitty Hawk* in 1903 that powered flight became a reality.

B That's what historians have always believed. However, a small minority of researchers and scientists have re-examined historical objects and have found evidence to suggest that humans achieved flight earlier than the 20th century. They argue that flight was discovered long ago, but the knowledge of the technology was lost.

C A strange flying object was found in 1898 in a tomb at Saqquara, Egypt and was later dated to around 200 BCE. As aeroplanes had not been 'invented' in the late 19th century, when the object was found, it was stored in a box marked 'wooden bird model' in the museum of Cairo. The object was later re-discovered by Dr Khalil Messiha, who considered the object so important that a special committee of leading scientists was established to study the object. As a result of their findings, the object was displayed in the museum of Cairo as a 'model aeroplane'.

The scientists found that the model was a very advanced form of glider, which will stay in the air almost by itself. The curved shape and size of the glider's wings are behind its ability to fly; a similar type of curved wings can be seen on Concorde and gave the plane maximum 'lift' without a reduction in speed.

D Admittedly, it is difficult to believe that a flying device with such advanced features was invented more than 2,000 years ago; historians insist that aeroplanes did not exist in those times. But this object seems to suggest otherwise, despite the refusal of unimaginative science to accept the evidence.

E Gold trinkets discovered in Central America and coastal areas of South America are further evidence of early flight. Estimated to belong to a period between 500 and 800 CE, these objects look very like modern aircraft or even spacecraft. The archaeologists who discovered them labelled these objects as *zoomorphic*, meaning 'animal shaped', but it is unclear which animal they represent. In fact, the structures on the objects look more mechanical, like the parts on an aeroplane. Photos of the objects were analysed by several experts. One of them was Arthur Young, a designer of Bell helicopters and other aircraft. His analysis confirmed that the object contains many features which would fit the aeroplane theory.

F In other cultures, flying vehicles are written about in early texts, such as the Indian epic, the *Mahábhárata* and other books such as *Bhágavata Purána* and *Rámáyana*. The flying devices were called *vimánas* and were discussed in *Vaimánika Shástra*, describing flying machines with different purposes and capabilities. The *Book of Enoch* not only describes flying machines but also spacecraft. There is no shortage of descriptions of flying machines in ancient sources. If we examine them in detail, we discover to our surprise that flying in ancient times seems to be the rule, not the exception.

Questions 1–6

Reading Passage 3 has six paragraphs, **A–F**. Choose the best headings for each paragraph from the list below.

> **List of headings**
>
> **i** 20th century flight
> **ii** Refusing to accept the evidence
> **iii** Is it a bird…or a plane?
> **iv** Re-writing history
>
> **v** Further evidence of early flight
> **vi** Written description of ancient flight
> **vii** The first powered planes
> **ix** A brief history of flight

1 Paragraph A		**2** Paragraph B		**3** Paragraph C	
4 Paragraph D		**5** Paragraph E		**6** Paragraph F	

Questions 7–14

Do the following statements agree with the information given in the reading passage above? Write:

TRUE   if the statement agrees with the information

FALSE   if the statement contradicts the information

NOT GIVEN   if there is no information on this

7 Powered flight was invented by the French in the late eighteenth century.
8 Most scientists believe that flight was discovered earlier than the 20th century.
9 Dr Khalil Messiha found the model aeroplane in an Egyptian tomb.
10 Scientists compared the Egyptian model aeroplane's wings to those of Concorde.
11 Science is open-minded about the possibility of early flying machines.
12 The gold objects were originally believed to be models of animals.
13 Arthur Young built a life-sized aeroplane based on the South American models.
14 Evidence of early flight can be found in old books.

Reading Passages 4, 5 and 6

Skills development

Using information in a table

In some exam questions you will have to complete a table with information from the passage. Sometimes the same word in the passage appears in the table.

1 a Find the word 'analysis' in the table.
b Scan the passage for the same word.
c Note down the word which is before 'analysis' in paragraphs B–E.
d Which column of the table names the type of analysis? Which row of the table does each paragraph refer to? Write the types of analysis in the table.

2 a Look at the first word in bold in the Method column of the table. Scan the relevant paragraph for a synonym of the word in bold.
b Scan the information around the synonym for other words which are in the sentence in the table.
c Look at the gap in the sentence and decide what type of word you need.
d Repeat steps **a–c** with the other words in bold in the table.

3 a Look at the first word in italics in the Advantages/Disadvantages column of the table.
b Think of different forms of the word, e.g. *analyze, analysis, analytical.*
c Scan the relevant paragraph for a different form of the word in italics.
d Look at the gap in the sentence and decide what type of word you need. Scan the relevant paragraph for this type of word.

Remember
In some exam questions you will have to complete a table with information from the passage. You need to bear in mind that sometimes the same word in the passage appears in the table but at other times, synonyms of important words are used. A different form of a word in the passage can also appear in the table.

4 Now complete the table below. Choose **NO MORE THAN ONE WORD** from the reading passage for each answer.

Type of analysis	Method	Advantages/Disadvantages
Expert	Style of **famous** artist matched to the (1) .... of the painting.	Limited: experts can't **date** (2) .... or see through paint.
(3)	Looked at (4) .... **below** Italian painting.	Forgers can (5) .... *discovery* by using authentic materials.
Canvas	(6) .... looks through layer of paint. (7) .... and pattern of threads counted.	It's *quick* and (8) ....
(9)	**Quantity** and (10) .... of strokes counted by a program.	

Reading Passage 4

The war against forgery

A Talented artists used to make thousands of pounds from 'forging' works of art. This involved painting a picture in the style of a famous artist and then selling it as an 'undiscovered' work by that artist. Forgery is an illegal practice but it is very difficult to prove. As a result, many galleries still believe they own forgeries. They hope that science will help them to identify whether their paintings are the real thing or fakes.

B In the past, galleries have relied on experts, who used their experience to analyze the look of a painting and decide whether it matched the style of a well-known artist. Expert analysis has limitations, however. The human eye cannot identify the age of the materials used, or see underneath the paint to the canvas that the artist painted on.

C Infrared analysis, in contrast, can do this. This scientific method was used by the National Gallery in London to prove that an Italian painting was not created by the famous 15th-century artist Francesco Francia but by a forger. By analyzing the painting with infrared, scientists discovered that the drawing underneath the painting was done in pencil, a material which wasn't available in the 15th century. Of course, it's possible for forgers to avoid being discovered by infrared analysis. They simply use materials which were available at the time that the original painting would have been created.

D Another scientific technique makes the forger's job more difficult. The method of canvas analysis has been developed by Professor C Richard Johnson. He uses X-ray to see through the paint layer. A computer program then counts the number and pattern of threads in the canvas and attempts to match them to a canvas of a famous painting. The reason behind this method is that some well-known painters such as Vincent van Gogh bought their canvas in a roll of material, which means that several van Goghs from the same period should have the same number and patterns of threads in the canvas. This type of analysis can be done quickly and is very accurate.

E Like Richard Johnson, Eric Postma, Professor of Artificial Intelligence at Tilburg University in the Netherlands uses computers to analyze paintings, but his approach focuses on the painting rather than the canvas. He has invented brush-stroke analysis. A computer program studies the colours used by a particular artist and counts the number and combination of brush strokes used across a paintings. If the number or style of brushstrokes differed in one painting to other paintings created by the same artist, Postma's team identified it as a fake.

F Computer analysis of art has been effective in identifying forgeries so far, but it's only a matter of time before the forgers find a way of avoiding discovery. However, Johnson believes that in the end, the scientists will win.

How vision works

A   Although the human eye is small, it is one of the most complicated organs in the body. It has many different parts and each one helps us to see; some parts receive light into the eye and some send electrical impulses, or messages, which communicate an image of what we are looking at to our brains.

B   Light first enters the eye through the cornea. This is the clear part of the eye which bends the light so that it is at the correct angle to pass through the pupil. The pupil is a black hole which allows light into the eye. It is in the middle of a coloured circle, called the iris. The iris makes the pupil reduce in size by contracting and enlarge by relaxing. The amount of light that goes into the eye is controlled by the changing size of the pupil in order for the sensitive parts at the back of the eye to be protected from damage.

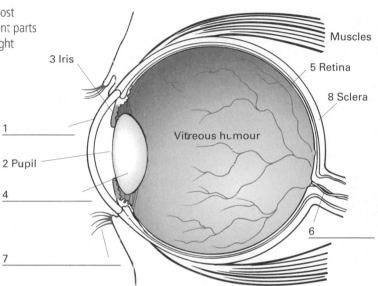

C   After passing through the pupil, the light enters the lens behind. The lens works rather like a camera lens, controlling the direction of the light so that it reaches the right place at the back of the eye. This area is called the retina. Before the light reaches the retina, however, it has to pass through the vitreous humour, in the middle of the eye.

D   The retina converts light into electrical messages, which are then sent to the brain along the optic nerve. Around the centre of the retina, there are light sensitive cells called cones. There are between 6 and 7 million cones in the human eye. They recognize colour and detail and need daylight to work well. Rods are sensitive to dark and light and do not recognize colours. They transmit black and white information to the brain. Rods outnumber cones; there are approximately 120 million of them in the eye. It is the rods which help us to 'see in the dark'.

E   The eye does not stay still; it needs to move up, down and across to allow us to see all around us. Six muscles attached to the sides of the eye and going behind it allow it to move at an angle of 180 degrees but prevent the eye rolling backwards. Because the eye is open to the outside world, small objects can fly into it. Eyelashes stop this from happening. The white layer around the outside of the eye, called the sclera, protects the delicate insides of the eye from danger by preventing small objects from getting into the eye.

Remember
- Use the information in the diagram to give you clues about the information you need to find in the text.
- Scan the passage for the words which are given in the diagram and read the text around them. Does it give you any important information?
- Look at where the parts of the diagram that you have to label are. Then scan the passage for words which describe location in the text e.g. *behind, in front of, between* etc.
- Think about the function of the parts of the diagram. Then scan the passage for verbs which describe a function.

1   Look at the diagram of the eye. How many labels do you have to complete? How many parts of the eye are already labelled?

2   Read the title of Reading Passage 5 and the first paragraph and answer the questions.

   1 Which verb in paragraph A relates to the word 'vision'?
   2 What two important jobs do the parts of the eye do?

3   Look at the completed labels on the diagram and choose the correct option in sentences **a–d**. Then scan the reading passage for information about these parts of the eye and check your answers.

   a The pupil is *on the outside / in the middle* of the iris.
   b The retina is *at the front / at the back* of the eye.
   c Muscles go *behind / in front of* the eye from the sides.
   d The sclera is on the *inside / outside* of the eye.

4 Match the parts of the eye mentioned in Exercise 3 to their function **A–E**.

    A controls the amount of light entering the eye
    B stop small objects flying into the eye
    C allows light into the eye
    D control the movement of the eye
    E converts light into electrical messages

5 Look again at the labels you have to complete on the diagram and answer the questions. Then scan the text to check your answers.

    1 How would you describe where the parts of the eye are?
    2 What do you think the function of each part of the eye is?

6 Label the diagram above. Choose **NO MORE THAN ONE WORD** from the passage for each answer.

Sentence completion: recognizing word class and synonyms

Remember
The exam instructions usually say 'Choose one word only from the passage for each answer.' or 'Choose no more than two/three words from the passage…' Make sure
- you use the same words as the words used in the passage when completing the sentences.
- you use no more than the number of words stated.
- the word you find is the correct word class (noun, adjective, verb etc.) so that the sentence is grammatically correct.

1 Read statements **1–5** in the exam question below. One word is missing from each sentence. Choose the correct type of word for each gap.
    a noun: plural or singular?
    b verb: past or present?

Complete the sentences below. Choose **ONE WORD ONLY** from the passage for each answer.

1 Cones don't <u>function efficiently</u> without ....
2 Rods .... information in <u>monochrome</u>.
3 There are <u>more rods</u> than .... on the retina.
4 .... <u>stop</u> the eye from rolling backwards.
5 Eyelashes protect the eye from <u>tiny airborne</u> ....

2 Exam questions often use different wording to the text. Find the phrases in the text that mean the same as the underlined phrases in **1–5**. Then find the words you need to fill in each gap.

3 Look at the example student's answers for statements 2 and 5. Are they correct or incorrect? Check that your answers to Exercise 2 use the same words as in the text.

2 Rods ....*send*........ information in <u>monochrome</u>.
5 Eyelashes protect the eye from <u>tiny airborne</u> ......*small things*...... .

Summary completion: passive sentences

1 Look at sentence **A** and the second sentence in the summary below. The subject of both sentences have been underlined. Answer the questions.

    1 Are the subjects of both sentences the same?

    2 Which sentence uses the present simple form of the main verb? Which sentence uses the verb *be* + a past participle?

    3 Which sentence is active and which is passive?

A <u>The amount of light that goes into the eye</u> is controlled by the changing size of the pupil in order for the sensitive parts at the back of the eye to be protected from damage.

The process of sight

Light enters the eye through the 1 .....*cornea*..... and then the pupil. <u>The changing size of the pupil</u> controls the quantity of light which enters the eye and therefore protects its sensitive parts at the back of the eye. By 2 .... and relaxing, the iris varies the size of the pupil. From the retina, the 3 .... sends electrical messages to the brain. Black and white information is transmitted to the brain by 4 .... The eye is protected both by our eyelashes and a 5 .... protective layer known as the sclera.

---

2 Compare sentences **2–5** in the summary to sentences **B–E** below. Underline the passive sentences or clauses.

    B The coloured part around the pupil, known as the iris, makes the pupil reduce in size by contracting and enlarge by relaxing.

    C The retina converts light into electrical messages, which are then sent to the brain along the optic nerve.

    D Rods are sensitive to dark and light and do not recognize colours. They transmit black and white information to the brain.

    E The white layer outside of the eye, called the sclera, protects the delicate insides of the eye from danger, preventing small objects from getting into the eye.

3 What type of words (noun, adjective, adverb etc.) do you need for each gap in the summary?

4 Now complete the summary. Choose **NO MORE THAN TWO WORDS** from the passage for each answer.

Remember
- There are two types of summary task. In one type, a list of words you need to fill in each gap are given in a box. These words also appear in the passage. There are always more words than you need.
- In the other type of summary task, you need to choose words from the passage to complete the summary.
- Sometimes only part of a text is summarized. Scan the passage for words in the title or the first line of the summary to help you find the section you need..
- Completion tasks normally state the number of words you will need to complete each gap. You will lose marks if you use more words than the task instruction states
- The order of sentences in the summary is not always the same as the order of information in the passage. Look for key words from the summary in the passage to help you find the correct information.

Now practise the skills you have learnt by answering the questions on Reading Passage 6.

Reading Passage 6

The history of chocolate

A   The history of chocolate started in South America and the Amazon. Ancient man picked the sweet fruit off the trees and ate it, throwing away the seeds. The pod of the cacao tree tasted sweet, like apricots, whereas the beans – or seeds – inside the pod were bitter. It's not known when ancient civilizations found out how to use the cacao's seeds. It might have been by accident, when the beans fell into a fire and roasted, releasing a chocolate-like smell – however, the use of cacao beans as a food probably took place during the time of the Olmecs.

B   The Olmecs (1200 to 300 BC) were an ancient tribe from South Central Mexico. They were the first to grow the cacao plant and use the beans. They had a name for these bitter seeds that held secrets to health and power: *kakawa*, or cacao.

C   Following the Olmecs, the Mayans treasured cacao as a medicine and a food. But they did not make chocolate bars. Instead, the beans were mixed with corn and flavourings to make savoury meals. These dishes were very bitter – very different from the chocolate we eat now.

D   Many years later, between the 14th and 16th centuries, the Aztecs used the cacao bean as their form of currency: in other words, beans were used like coins. A list of Aztec trading prices looked something like this:
1 small rabbit = 30 cacao beans
1 turkey egg = 3 cacao beans
1 large tomato = 1 cacao bean

E   Christopher Columbus saw how the people of South America valued the beans, but he thought they were a type of nut – an almond. Although he brought cacao beans back to Spain with him nobody knew what they were or what to do with them.

F   Then, in 1519, Hernan Cortes arrived at the great court of the Aztec king, Montezuma. He and his crew saw how the Aztecs used chocolate. Cortes himself didn't enjoy the Aztecs' bitter brew, but he recognized its value. He wrote to King Carlos I of Spain that chocolate was a 'drink that builds up resistance and fights fatigue'.

G   After the Spanish conquered the Aztecs and began building settlements in the New World, they adopted many of the foods of the native people, including chocolate. European immigrants to the New World brought sugar and other foods to South and Central America, and the Spanish settlers began drinking chocolate hot and sweet.

H   It took a royal wedding to make chocolate a star in Europe. When the Spanish princess, Maria Theresa, came to the French court at Versailles to marry King Louis XIV in 1660, she brought her precious cacao beans with her. Hot chocolate was served at the wedding and the bride's guests loved it. Although chocolate was expensive its popularity spread in France and England. Hot chocolate was served in 'chocolate houses,' not unlike the cafés you see on every street corner today.

I   The 19th-century Industrial Revolution saw inventions that changed the nature of chocolate, particularly in Switzerland. For example, Swiss chemist Henri Nestlé invented a process to create powdered milk, and together with Daniel Peter, a chocolate manufacturer, he created the very first milk chocolate bar in 1879. In the same year, Rudolphe Lindt invented the conche machine and the process known as 'conching' which made shiny, smooth and creamy chocolate. These advances made the Swiss the leaders of chocolate manufacturing, and throughout the 19th century they produced 12,000 pounds of chocolate per Swiss citizen per year, most of it for export.

1 Complete the flow chart. Choose **ONE WORD ONLY** from the passage for each answer.

The history of chocolate

South America and the Amazon: (1) _____ eaten but not beans.

South Central Mexico: (2) _____ the first to use the beans.

Mayans used beans in (3) _savoury_ dishes. (bitter, not sweet)

Beans used as a type of (4) _currency_ – to buy and sell things.

Columbus brought cacao beans to Spain and Cortes recognized health properties.

Europeans brought sugar to the New World.

Spanish in New World started to drink (5) _sweet and_ hot chocolate.

Chocolate introduced to Europe during a (6) _wedding._

Hot chocolate drunk in (7) _Chocolate houses._

2 Complete the sentences below. Write **NO MORE THAN THREE WORDS** for each answer.

were bitter (South America)

1 Although the seeds of the cacao plant were bitter, the pod had a taste similar to _apricots._

2 Ancient civilizations may have discovered how to use the cacao's seeds by _accident._

3 To the Aztecs, one _____ was worth thirty cacao beans.

4 Maria Theresa's _guest_ enjoyed hot chocolate when she got married.

5 Chocolate was popular in Europe, despite it being _____ _of real_

3 Complete the summary of paragraph I with the list of words **A–H** below.

A chocolate bars	B consumed	C exported	D inventions
E machine	F manufacturer	G powdered	H process

The birth of chocolate bars

Switzerland was responsible for many of the 6 _D_ that redefined chocolate and they became leading chocolate manufacturers. Henri Nestlé made 7 _powdered_ milk. He then collaborated with Daniel Peter to make 8 _A_ . Chocolate was made smoother through a 9 _machine_ called conching, invented by Lindt. Most of the chocolate that was made in Switzerland was 10 _export_ .

GREEN CHINA?

A Rizhao, in Shandong Province, is one of the hundreds of Chinese cities <u>preparing to get much bigger.</u> The road into town is eight lanes wide, even though at the moment there's not much traffic. But the port is very busy; large quantities of iron arrive every day by ship. Rizhao is the kind of place which environmental scientists are worried about: China's economic development has led to a high number of new building projects taking place throughout the country. The growth of cities increases the amount of harmful greenhouse gas released into the atmosphere. It's this kind of expansion that has increased the production of global warming gases in China.

B However, cities like Rizhao are taking steps to counteract the damage the gases are causing. On top of 95% of the buildings in the city, there are solar panels, which use energy from the sun to power the city's hotels, shops and houses. And it's not just Rizhao which is spending money on environmentally friendly energy, the whole of China is number 1 in the world for using renewable energy technology.

C China is doing its best to stop using [1]<u>oil, coal and gas</u> – which harm the environment – and start depending only on 'clean' *energy* such as sun and wind power. This change is not easy to make because of the **need to develop** [2]<u>quickly.</u> China's economy *needs to grow* at least 8% a year to ensure social stability; the government's hope is to keep producing enough [3]<u>fresh employment opportunities</u> for the [4]<u>growing</u> [5]<u>populations</u> of the new cities. Better jobs mean [6]<u>greater wealth</u> and people in the cities are *spending their money* on technology. The average Shanghainese household already has 1.9 air conditioners, not to mention 1.2 computers. People in Beijing **buy** 20,000 new cars a month. As of 2007, China had 22 cars for every 1,000 people, compared with 451 in the USA. Of course, this means that the [7]<u>demand for **power**</u> is increasing.

D China's interests in technology could, however, provide a part of the solution to the environmental problem. Because it's putting up so many new buildings and power plants, the country can include the latest environmentally-friendly technology. In time the technology should reduce the amount of carbon released into the atmosphere.

E This reduction will probably not be enough to stop dramatic global warming though. Scientists predict that carbon levels will continue to rise until the year 2030, which will cause the earth to heat up enough to melt the Himalayan glaciers and to cause the seas to rise. It's a dark picture. Stopping global warming needs international collaboration. Other large countries need to take steps to be more green, the USA for example. In the end, no one country can take full responsibility for saving the environment; we are all responsible.

Multiple choice questions: reading the question

1 Read questions **1–3** in the tables below and on page 33.
Where can you find the correct answer to each question in the passage?
Whose thoughts and opinions are important in questions 2 and 3?

2 Read question **1** and options **A–D** and answer questions **i–v** on the right. Then decide which option **A–D** is correct.

1 According to paragraph A, China has environmental problems because	i Which of these questions is similar in meaning to question 1? 'Why is the environment improving?' 'Why is there damage to the environment?'
A the city of Rizhao has recently expanded	ii Look at the underlined words in the paragraph. Does this agree with statement c? Does the paragraph say more about Rizhao's development or China's development?
B the roads are getting bigger	iii Find a reference to roads in Rizhao. Is there a link in the paragraph between the roads and greenhouse gases?
C it's importing raw materials, like iron.	iv Find a reference to iron. Does the paragraph say what effect iron has on the environment?
D the development of cities is releasing greenhouse gases.	v Does the passage link development and greenhouse gases? How does the writer describe the gases?

3 Read question **2** and options **A–D** and answer questions **i–v** on the right. Then decide which option **A–D** is correct.

2 What is the writer's purpose in paragraph B?	**i** Which of these has a similar meaning to 'purpose'? *a reason / an opinion about something*
A to talk about environmental problems in China.	**ii** Does the paragraph give examples of environmental problems?
B to demonstrate that Rizhao is environmentally friendly.	**iii** Does 'environmentally friendly' have a positive or negative meaning? What kind of environmentally friendly energy is mentioned? Does the paragraph only talk about Rizhao?
C to give examples of China's economic development.	**iv** How many words connected with the economy can you find in the paragraph?
D to emphasize what China does to protect the environment.	**v** How many examples can you find of China protecting the environment?

4 Read question **3** and options **A–D** and answer questions **i–v** on the right. Then decide which option **A–D** is correct.

3 According to paragraph E, how does the writer feel about the future of the environment?	**i** Which time word is in the question? Which date is referred to in the paragraph?
A optimistic	**ii** Which of these is similar to 'optimistic'? *excited / worried*
B hopeless	**iii** Does the writer offer any solutions to the environmental problems?
C pessimistic	**iv** Find a sentence in the paragraph which suggests the writer is concerned about the scientist's predictions.
D disinterested	**v** Does the final line of paragraph E suggest that the writer is interested in the problem of global warming?

Recognizing synonyms

1 Read the question. How many correct answers are there?

Which **THREE** reasons explain why it is difficult to solve China's environmental problems?

A The number of people living in the countryside is increasing.

not correct. The paragraph says the population of the cities is growing.

B There's a shortage of fossil fuels.

C The economy needs new jobs to be created.

D Chinese with more money want to buy energy-hungry machines.

E China is developing rapidly.

2 Match the underlined key words in options **A–E** to the underlined words which have a similar meaning in paragraph **C** of the reading passage.

3 Look at the phrases in *italics*. Which words in **bold** are they similar to?

4 Read around the words in bold and decide which options are not correct.

A SHORT HISTORY OF THE GREAT DEPRESSION

The Great Depression was a worldwide economic crisis. The USA was badly affected, suffering unemployment, greatly reduced industrial production and building, and an 89 percent decline in stock prices. Before the depression, in the 1920s, the USA enjoyed a time of low unemployment and economic health, although there was a big gap between the rich and poor.

October 29th 1929 marked the start of the Depression. 'Black Tuesday' was the day when stock market shares fell almost 23 percent and the market lost between $8 billion and $9 billion in value. But it was just one in a series of losses over a period of time which put stockbrokers and bankers who had bought shares with borrowed money in danger of losing everything.

As the depression continued in the USA, the stock market value continued to decline. Unemployment rose and wages fell for those who continued to work. Those who had bought homes, cars, furniture and household appliances with borrowed money – on credit – had to give them back. As consumers lost buying power industrial production fell, businesses failed, and more workers lost their jobs. The depression also hit farmers hard. A dramatic fall in food prices, loss of exports and years of no rain made it impossible to make a profit. As people living in cities lost their homes, farmers also lost their land.

The government did little to help. President Herbert Hoover believed the government should watch the economy carefully and encourage consumer spending but he did not want to do more. As unemployment rose, he refused to offer money or create jobs.

By 1932 the unemployment rate had grown to more than 20 percent. Thousands of banks and businesses had failed. Millions were homeless. Men (and women) returned home from unsuccessful job hunts to find their homes locked and their possessions and families on the streets. Many people lived at the edges of cities in temporary 'towns' and had to find food where they could.

In 1933, when President Roosevelt was elected, he faced a banking crisis and unemployment that had reached 24.9 percent. Thirteen to 15 million workers had no jobs. Roosevelt offered a series of emergency actions which were seen as a 'new deal for the American people.' During his first 100 days as president, he changed the banking system and improved the stock market, protected home owners, tried to make industrial and agricultural production more stable, set up building projects to create jobs and donated government money to millions of people.

Roosevelt's New Deal removed the worst effects of the Great Depression but the economy in the USA didn't recover completely until 1954.

Glossary
depression = a period of time when there is a lot of unemployment and poverty because there is very little economic activity
crisis = a difficult or dangerous situation
decline = to become less or worse
borrow = to receive and use something that belongs to someone else, and promise to give it back to them later e.g. I borrowed money from the bank.
consumers = people who buy and use goods or services
temporary = existing for only a limited period of time
stable = not changing frequently and not likely to become worse
recover = to begin to get stronger and return to its earlier state

Matching features: recognizing paraphrasing

1 Underline dates **A–E** below in the passage and choose the correct option in this sentence:

In matching tasks, the categories are in *the same* / *a different* order to the order they appear in the passage.

    A 1920s
    B 1929
    C 1932
    D 1933
    E 1954

2 Look at the statements **1–3** and the matching sentences **A–C** from the passage. Underline words which are the same or have a similar meaning.

1 One fifth of the population were without work.

    A By ... the unemployment rate had grown to more than 20 percent.

2 New jobs were created and the banking system was changed.

    B he changed the banking system ... set up building projects to create jobs ...

3 The economic situation in the USA improved.

    C ... the economy in the USA didn't recover completely until 1954.

3 How are statements **1–3** different to sentences **A–C**? For each pair of sentences choose the correct paraphrasing technique **i–iii** from the box.

i changing an active sentence in the passage into a passive sentence.
ii using synonyms and putting words in a different order in a sentence.
iii using a positive statement when the information in the passage uses negative forms.

4 Match each statement with the correct date. You may use any letter more than once.

    1 One fifth of the population were without work.
    2 New jobs were created and the banking system was changed.
    3 The economic situation in the USA improved.
    4 The stock market crashed.
    5 Millions of people lost their homes.
    6 There was enough money and jobs for people.
    7 Farmers suffered due to bad weather and falling food prices.

A 1920s
B 1929
C 1932
D 1933
E 1954

Now practise the skills you have learnt by answering the questions on Reading Passage 9.

Reading Passage 9

Coming to TV screens of the future: A sense of smell

A research breakthrough toward odor-generating TV

A   Today's television programs are designed to trigger your emotions and your mind through your senses of sound and sight. But what if they could trigger your sense of smell? What if you could smell or taste the cheesy slices of pizza being eaten by your favourite characters on TV? Is it possible? Would audiences enjoy the experience? Would advertisers jump on the opportunity to reach consumers in a new way?

B   These questions formed the basis of a two year experiment by researchers at the University of California, San Diego who worked with Samsung Advanced Institute of Technology (SAIT) in Korea. In a proof of concept paper published this month in the journal *Angewandte Chemie*, the researchers demonstrate that it is possible to generate thousands of odors, on demand, using a device small enough to fit on the back of your TV. 'For example, if people are eating pizza, the viewer smells pizza coming from a TV or cell phone,' said Sungho Jin, professor in the departments of Mechanical and Aerospace Engineering and NanoEngineering at the UC San Diego Jacobs School of Engineering. 'And if a beautiful lady walks by, they smell perfume. Instantaneously generated fragrances or odors would match the scene shown on a TV or cell phone, and that's the idea.'

D   The scent comes from a liquid solution such as ammonia, which forms a smelly gas when heated through a thin metal wire by an electrical current. The solution is kept in a silicone compartment. As the heat and odor pressure build, a tiny compressed hole in the compartment is opened, releasing the odor.

E   Whether TV and cell phone audiences and advertisers will respond to such idea are questions for another phase of the study. Certainly when the idea of smell-o-vision (known then as 'scentovision') first hit our cinema screens and noses in 1950s, it wasn't very popular with cinema audiences. However, the idea of smell-o-vision has staying power.

F   The UCSD team tested their device with two commercially available perfumes, Live by Jennifer Lopez, and Passion by Elizabeth Taylor. In both cases, a human tester was able to smell and distinguish the scents within 30 centimeters of the test chamber. When the perfumes were switched, the tester was exposed to coffee beans, which is commonly used to clear a tester's sense of smell in perfume development.

G   The next steps in the research would include developing a prototype and demonstrating that it is reliable enough to release odors on demand. It will also need to be increased and decreased in size in order to fit consumer electronics like TVs and cell phones. And there are a few other considerations. For example, perfume companies might like you to smell their latest scents through TV, but scientists have yet to think of a way that these could be transmitted to the device. 'That's a logistics problem', said Jin. 'But in specific applications one can always think of a way.'

H   Certainly, if a solution is found, advertisers will have yet another means of persuading consumers to purchase their products. Films too, could take advantage of the invention, perhaps even matching smells to their character's personality. One can't help wondering whether smell-o-vision would always be desirable, however. Whilst it may be enjoyable to smell the recipe created by a TV chef, a nature programme or a horror film may not produce such pleasant odors. One can only hope that the UCSD team will invent a means of switching smell-o-vision off.

1   Choose the correct letter, **A, B, C** or **D**.

   1 According to paragraph B, what can the device do?
     A release a smell when the viewer asks it to
     B release a smell that matches what the viewer is eating
     C release a smell which matches the scene on TV
     D release a smell after a delay of a few minutes

   2 What are the similarities between 'odor-generating TV' and the development of perfume?
     A Both use the chemical ammonia.
     B Both use famous people in their testing procedures.
     C Both use human testers with a good sense of smell.
     D Coffee beans are used between smells.

   3 According to paragraph H, what is the writer's opinion of odor-generating TV?
     A enthusiastic
     B mixed
     C negative
     D irritated

2   Choose **FIVE** letters, **A–G**.

   Which **FIVE** aspects of odor-generating TV need more research?

     A how to switch odor-generating TV off and on
     B how popular odor-generating TV will be with consumers
     C whether the device can be relied upon to release smells instantly
     D whether the odor-releasing mechanism works
     E how far away from the TV or cell phone the smell can be detected
     F whether the size of the device can be changed
     G how smells can be transmitted from companies who want to market products

3   Classify the following statements as referring to

     A the proof of concept paper.
     B the concept of smell-o-vision.
     C the odor-generating TV device.
     D the prototype.

     1 This will be tested to establish its reliability.
     2 This isn't new and wasn't originally very successful.
     3 This will need to be adapted for consumer products.
     4 This is the product of two years of research.
     5 This works through heating scented liquid.
     6 This was originally known as 'scentavision'.
     7 This was recently released in print.

How much do you know about the IELTS Academic Writing module? Do the quiz below to find out.

Quiz

1 Complete the sentences with the correct numbers from the box.

20	250	60	150	40

1 The Writing Module lasts for .... minutes.
2 You should spend .... minutes on Task 1.
3 You should spend .... minutes on Task 2.
4 You should write at least .... words for Task 1.
5 You should write at least .... words for Task 2.

2 Complete the table with three task types.
A an essay giving opinions
B a description of an event
C a description of a photograph
D a description of a process

E a formal letter of application
F a description of data in a graph, chart or table.

Task 1	Task 2

3 Choose four correct answers.
You get more marks if you
A have neat handwriting.
B use correct grammar and spelling.
C write a lot more than the number of words suggested.
D use a variety of vocabulary.
E answer all parts of the question.
F include as much detail as possible.
G organize your ideas clearly.

Writing Task 1

Remember
When you describe a graph in the exam, think carefully about what information you need to include. Don't include every detail of the information – you need to select the most important information that describes trends, differences or stages.

Skills development

Understanding graphs: choosing the most important information

In Writing Task 1 you will be asked to describe data in a chart, graph or table.

1 Look at the bar graph and decide if the statements are *True*, *False* or *Not Given*.

a The numbers up the vertical axis are percentages.
b The graph shows changes over time.
c People in England generally earn more than people in Scotland.
d People in all the UK countries earned more in 2010 than they did 9 years before.
e People in Wales earned about ten pounds less in 2010 than in 2007.
f Weekly earnings in England are the highest out of all the countries in the UK.
g In the year 2001, in England the average amount earned per week was about 100 pounds more than the amount earned in Wales in the same year.

2 Which four statements, **c–g**, describe the most important information in the graph? Which describe less important detail?

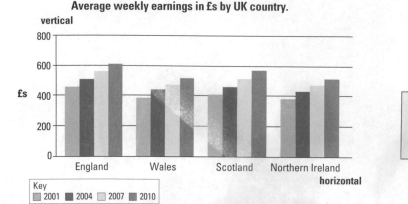

Average weekly earnings in £s by UK country.

Glossary
earning/wage = amount of money that a person takes home for working

Describing data

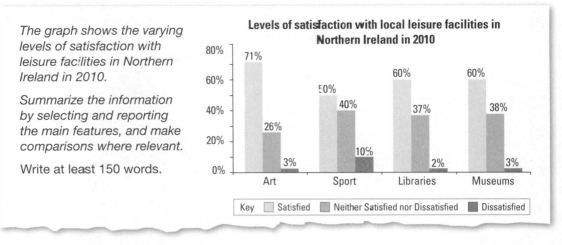

The graph shows the varying levels of satisfaction with leisure facilities in Northern Ireland in 2010.

Summarize the information by selecting and reporting the main features, and make comparisons where relevant.

Write at least 150 words.

Levels of satisfaction with local leisure facilities in Northern Ireland in 2010

Key: Satisfied · Neither Satisfied nor Dissatisfied · Dissatisfied

1 Look at the graph above and read the exam question. Then complete the example answer below with words **A–E**. You will need to use the words more than once.

A level   **B** percentage   **C** area   **D** levels   **E** percent

This graph shows the different ¹.................... of satisfaction felt by people in Northern Ireland about art, sport, library and museum facilities in their local area.

Overall, the ².................... of people who were satisfied with their local facilities was high. ³.................... of satisfaction with all types of facility were **higher** than 45 ⁴.................... . ⁵.................... of dissatisfaction were **much** lower, ranging from the **lowest** at two ⁶.................... to the highest, with sports facilities, at ten ⁷.................... .

⁸.................... of satisfaction were highest with arts facilities, at **just over** 70 ⁹.................... . The response to libraries and museums was **a little less** positive, with 60 ¹⁰.................... of people feeling satisfied with these facilities. The lowest ¹¹.................... of satisfaction was with sports facilities, with 50 ¹².................... of people feeling satisfied.

Interestingly, the ¹³.................... of people who didn't feel strongly about their local facilities was **quite high**, particularly in the ¹⁴.................... of sport. 40 ¹⁵.................... of people were neither dissatisfied nor satisfied with their sports facilities – only ten ¹⁶.................... fewer than those who were satisfied.

2 Look at the words in bold in the description and answer the questions.

   A Which word is a superlative adjective? e.g. *tallest*
   B Which adverb means 'a lot'? (used with a comparative)
   C Which word is a comparative adjective? e.g. *bigger*
   D Which word has a similar meaning to 'generally'?
   E Which three words means 'slightly'? (used with a comparative or an adjective)

3 Read the example answer again and circle the correct answer.

   1 The example answer includes *all / some* of the numbers in the graph.
   2 Numbers are included *before / after* a statement is made about the graph.
   3 Numbers support *important / all* points, for example, the biggest or smallest piece of information.

Remember
When you describe a graph, support important points with numbers from the graph. Important points could be the biggest or smallest piece of information, or – in graphs that show changes over time – where a trend reaches its highest amount or 'peaks'. Sometimes graphs use different symbols to indicate different quantities, e.g. % = percent or £ = pounds. High numbers are sometimes used e.g. 100,000 = one hundred thousand. You need to know how to write these in full.

Structuring a chart description

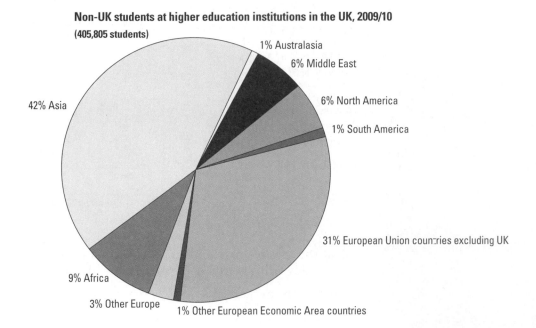

Non-UK students at higher education institutions in the UK, 2009/10
(405,805 students)

1% Australasia
6% Middle East
6% North America
1% South America
31% European Union countries excluding UK
1% Other European Economic Area countries
3% Other Europe
9% Africa
42% Asia

1 Look at the chart above. Match the percentages **1–4** to the places in the chart **A–D**.

1 ... ranging between six and nine percent
2 Together, these constitute 73 percent
3 ... at just over 40 percent
4 ... at just over 30%

A Asia and countries of the European Union
B countries of the European Union
C the Middle East, North America and Africa
D Asia

2 Complete these statements with the percentages **1–4** above.

A The percentage of students coming from continents such as Africa, North America and the Middle East was much lower, ... The smallest percentage of students come from South America and Australia, at 1%.
B This pie chart shows where the international students studying at colleges and universities in the United Kingdom come from.
C The majority of students come from Asia and countries in the European Union. .... of just over four hundred thousand international students who attend British higher education institutions.
D The highest percentage of international students in the UK came from Asia,

....

Countries from the European Union contributed the second highest percentage of international students ....

3 Put the statements describing the pie chart (**A–D**) from Exercise 2 into the following order:

1 A description of the subject of the graph (introduction).
2 The most important piece of data in the graph.
3 More details of the data in the graph, going from bigger to smaller.
4 The concluding sentence, describing the general trend.

Study Skills: Writing

Writing an introduction to a graph description

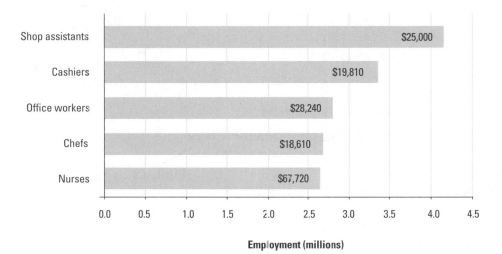

Average annual wages for occupations in the USA

1   Compare this introductory statement with the title of the graph above. Which words in the title have a similar meaning to the underlined words in the statement?
This graph shows the average <u>amount of money earned</u> by employees with particular <u>jobs</u> in the USA <u>every year</u>.

2   Match the titles of the graph **1–4** to the example introductory statements **A–D**.

Graph titles	Opening statements
1 Proportion of students who **graduated** in each **discipline** in **higher education** in Brazil.	A This graph shows the percentage of men and women who could read and write around the world.
2 Percentage of people who **participated** in the arts in Australia in 2010.	B This graph shows the average amount of electricity needed every three months.
3 **Global** adult **literacy rate** according to both genders.	C This pie chart shows the percentage of students who completed their studies of particular subjects at university in Brazil.
4 **Typical quarterly** demand for electricity.	D This graph shows the number of people who took part in the arts in Australia in 2010.

3   Underline the words in the opening statements which mean the same as the words in bold in the titles.

Skills practice

Study the chart and the exam question. Write four sentences to describe the information.

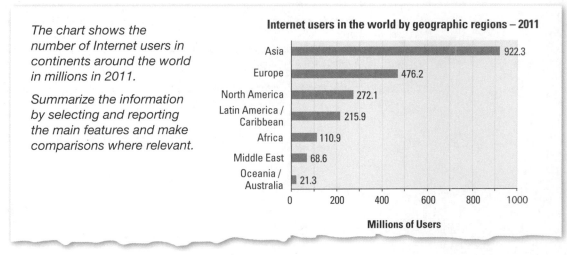

The chart shows the number of Internet users in continents around the world in millions in 2011.

Summarize the information by selecting and reporting the main features and make comparisons where relevant.

Internet users in the world by geographic regions – 2011

Asia — 922.3
Europe — 476.2
North America — 272.1
Latin America / Caribbean — 215.9
Africa — 110.9
Middle East — 68.6
Oceania / Australia — 21.3

Millions of Users

Skills development

Describing changes over time

Figure 1

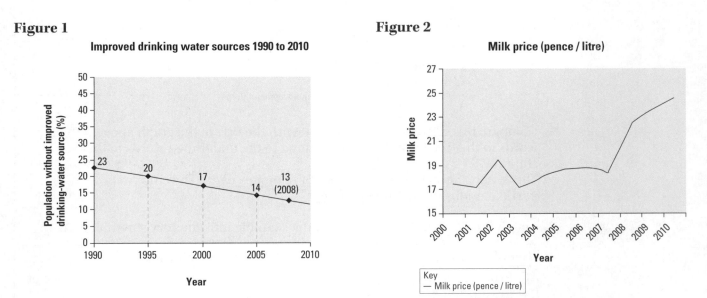

Improved drinking water sources 1990 to 2010

Population without improved drinking-water source (%)

23, 20, 17, 14, 13 (2008)

Year

Figure 2

Milk price (pence / litre)

Milk price

Year

Key
— Milk price (pence / litre)

Figure 3

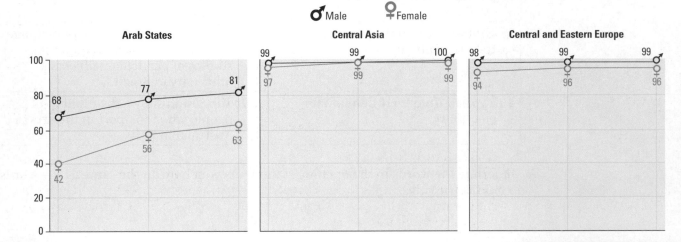

Adult literacy rate by sex and region, 1990–2008

♂ Male   ♀ Female

Arab States
68, 77, 81
42, 56, 63

Central Asia
99, 99, 100
97, 99, 99

Central and Eastern Europe
98, 99, 99
94, 96, 96

1 Match sentences **A–C** to figures **1–3**.

   A In Central Asia and Central and Eastern Europe, there was a **slight increase** in levels of literacy among women between 1990 and 1999, then rates overall **remained stable**. In the Arab states, however, there was a **steady rise** in literacy throughout the 18-year period.

   B ¹ The graph shows a **steady decline** in the number of people in the world who do not have clean water to drink. ² Between 1990 and 1995 there was **a fall** of three per cent and the same fall occurred between 1995 and 2000.

   C There was **a fluctuation** in the cost of milk over a period of eight years; there was a peak in prices in 2002, then after 2008, there was **a sharp rise**.

2 Look at sentences **A–C** above and complete column 2 of the table with the language in bold.

	(Adjective +) noun	Verb (+ adverb / adjective)
↗	a rise / an	to rise
↘	a .... / a decline	to fall
↑		
↘		
→	–	*to remain stable*
→		
↗		
∧∨∧∨↗		

Remember

Use an adjective + noun combination with *There is / there was* e.g. *In 1990 there was a steady rise in …* Try to vary your description; use adjective + noun combinations as well as verb + adverbs / adjectives combinations.

3 Complete column 3 of the table with the verbs, adverbs and adjectives in bold in **E–G**.

   E The number of people in the world who do not have clean water to drink **has declined steadily** since 1990. Between 1990 and 1995 the percentage fell by 3% and the same fall occurred between 1995 and 2000.

   F The cost of milk per litre **fluctuated** over a period of ten years but **rose dramatically** from 2008.

   G The percentage of women who can read and write in Central Asia and Central and Eastern Europe **increased slightly** between 1990 and 1999, then **remained stable**, whereas levels of literacy in the Arab states **rose steadily** over the period of 18 years.

Comparing data to show change

Leading exporters of clothing

Percentage change in world exports

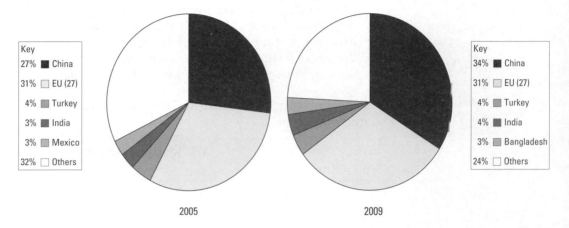

2005   2009

1 Look at the pair of pie charts above and put sentences **A–D** in the following order:

    1 An introductory sentence to the pie charts.
    2 The biggest growth and decrease in the pie charts.
    3 The smallest growth/decrease.
    4 Concluding sentence.

    A The two biggest changes which took place were in China and 'other countries'.
    B Between the years 2005 and 2009, China overtook the EU nations to become the biggest exporter of clothes worldwide in 2009.
    C Changes in clothing exports in other countries were small, or there was no change at all.
    D The two pie charts show how exports of clothing changed worldwide between two years: 2005 and 2009.

2 Sentences **1–5** below give information which supports the information in sentences **A–D** above. Match supporting sentences **1–5** to sentences **A–D**. Not all the sentences **A–D** have a supporting sentence, and some have more than one.

    1 India, for example, increased its clothing exports from three to four percent; a growth of one percent only.
    2 China's share of clothing exports increased the most of all the countries, from 27 to 34 percent. 'Other countries' share of clothing exports decreased by eight percent.
    3 There were no changes in Turkey's clothing exports; these stayed at four percent.
    4 Clothing exports from the 27 countries of the European Union also remained stable, at 31 percent in 2005 and 2009.

Remember

Organize your graph description. Group data so that each paragraph in the main body describes a particular change or pattern. Usually the first sentence of each paragraph introduces the change and other sentences in the paragraph support the first sentence with further detail from the graph.

Comparing two sets of data

The pie chart shows the journey time from home to work by percentage of the UK workforce. The table shows the journey times from home to work for workers living in London and those living in the rest of the UK.

Summarize the information by selecting and reporting the main features, and make comparisons where relevant.

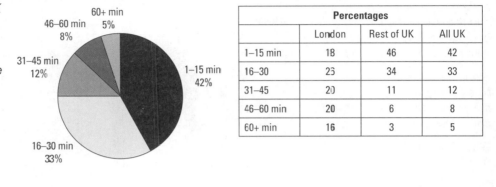

Percentage of workers by home-to-work travel time, October–December 2009, UK

Commuting times for workers living in London and the rest of the UK, in October–December 2009

Percentages			
	London	Rest of UK	All UK
1–15 min	18	46	42
16–30	25	34	33
31–45	20	11	12
46–60 min	20	6	8
60+ min	16	3	5

1 Look at the exam question above and choose the best opening statement, **A–C**.

    A These two sets of data detail the percentage of the UK population who travel for differing amounts of time in order to reach their place of employment.

    B These two sets of data compare the differing journey times undertaken by commuters in the UK in order to reach their place of work.

    C These two sets of data compare the journey times of commuters in the UK as a whole to those of commuters living in London.

2 In what order do you think you should describe the data in the graphs? Choose the best answer **A–C**. Then check your answer with the description of the graph below.

    A Describe all of the percentages in the pie chart and then compare them to all the percentages in the table.

    B Describe the key piece(s) of information in the UK and then compare it to the key piece(s) of information in London.

    C Describe all percentages in London travel times and then compare these to the key piece(s) of information in the rest of the UK.

Remember
- Don't try to include everything in both graphs; you need to summarize the most important information.
- Identify the most important information e.g. a general pattern or a change and describe it in the introduction.
- Use linkers to highlight contrasting information in your writing.
- Use pronouns to avoid repeating information – it makes your writing easier to read, e.g.: *These two sets of data compare the journey times of commuters in the UK as a whole to ~~the journey times~~* **those** *of commuters living in London.*

These two sets of data compare the journey times of commuters in the UK as a whole to those of commuters living in London.

Looking at the pie chart which relates to the UK as a whole, around three in four, or 75 per cent of workers take half an hour or less to travel from home to work, and 42% take less than a quarter of an hour.

However, the journey times of workers in London are very different to those of workers in the rest of the UK. People working in London tend to travel longer to get to work, with more than half of them, 56 per cent, commuting for more than thirty minutes to get to work every day. In contrast, of those working in the rest of the UK, only 20 per cent need to travel this long to reach their workplace.

To sum up, the majority of workers outside of London live within 30 minutes travelling time of their place of work, whereas the opposite can be said of the employees living in London.

3 Find three linking expressions which signal a contrast between two pieces of information. Which two of the expressions go at the beginning of a sentence?

The table shows the amount of time that workers spend getting to work in London and the rest of the UK. The bar chart shows the hourly earnings of the same workers.

Summarize the information by selecting and reporting the main features, and make comparisons where relevant.

Write at least 150 words.

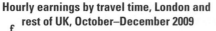

Hourly earnings by travel time, London and rest of UK, October–December 2009

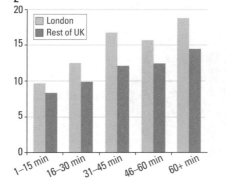

Commuting times for workers living in London and the rest of the UK, in October–December 2009

	Percentages		
	London	Rest of UK	All UK
1–15 min	18	46	42
16–30	26	34	33
31–45	20	11	12
46–60 min	20	6	8
60+ min	16	3	5

Remember

You will sometimes have to describe a diagram which shows a cycle in Writing Task 1. A cycle is a continuous process which doesn't have a start or an ending. You will need to decide the best starting point for your description.

Skills development

Organizing your writing

1 Look at the diagram which shows the water cycle and read the description below. Which place in the diagram does the description start from?

The diagram shows the cycle of water around the environment and its conversion from liquid into gas.

Summarize the information by selecting and reporting the main features and make comparisons where relevant.

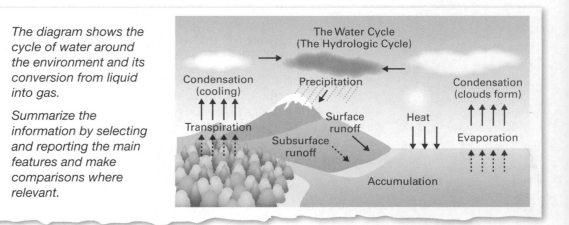

Remember

Use linking words to connect the different stages of your information. They will make your writing easier to read and will gain you more marks if you use them correctly.
You don't need to have special knowledge in order to describe a diagram.
Any technical vocabulary that you need will be written on the diagram.

The diagram illustrates the movement of water around our environment and the way it changes from a liquid, into a gas and then back into a liquid once more.

When water is heated by the sun, it evaporates from the ocean into the atmosphere. It also rises into the atmosphere from plants and trees. This process is called transpiration.

As the water rises into the atmosphere it cools and forms clouds. This process is called condensation.

Eventually, the water in the clouds falls back down to earth. This is called precipitation.

Some of the water goes into the ground and *after that*, runs into the seas and lakes. This is called subsurface runoff. Some of the water runs straight from the surface of the ground into the seas and lakes. The rest of the water is used by trees and plants.

Once the water reaches the seas, lakes and forests, the process of evaporation starts again.

2 Read the description again and decide if the statements are *True* or *False*.

    1 You should use different wording in the introductory sentence from the title of the diagram and from the exam question.

    2 You shouldn't separate stages of the diagram into different paragraphs.

    3 You don't need a concluding sentence which describes a general pattern.

3 Match the linking words in *italics* in the description to definitions **A–D** below.

    A Two words which describe things happening at the same time.

    B An expression which means the same as 'then'.

    C A word which means the same as 'after'.

    D A word which has a similar meaning to 'after a period of time'.

Choosing between the active and passive

1 Read sentences **A–C** below, from the description of the water cycle, and underline the verbs in each sentence. Then answer the questions.

    1 Which verbs are in the passive? (verb form of *be* + past participle)

    2 What is the subject of each sentence: the sun, water, trees and plants, or clouds?

    3 What is the most important thing in the description: the sun, water, trees and plants, or clouds?

    A *When* water is heated by the sun, it evaporates from the ocean into the atmosphere. It also rises into the atmosphere from plants and trees.

    B *Eventually*, the water in the clouds falls back down to earth.

    C The water is used by trees and plants.

Glass making process

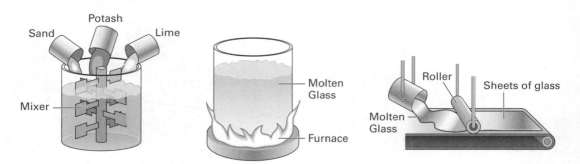

2 Look at the diagram of the glass making process and choose the best sentence **a** or **b**.

    1 a First of all, people mix sand, potash and lime in a large container.
       b First of all, sand, potash and lime are mixed together in a large container.

    2 a Then a furnace heats the sand, potash and lime until they melt into molten glass.
       b Then the sand, potash and lime are heated until they melt into molten glass.

    3 a Rollers make the glass into thin sheets, which are then cooled.
       b The molten glass is rolled into thin sheets, which are then cooled.

Describing a map

There are two types of map that you may need to describe in the exam.
1 A map that shows two or more possible locations for something.
2 A map that shows development of an area.

With both types of map, you need to paraphrase the exam instructions to sum up what the map shows (i.e. use different words to the exam question).

- With a map that shows two possible locations, you need to describe the main difference between the two locations. You then need to compare the two sites in detail and how they relate to other things on the map. You can state which site would be better and give reasons why this might be.

- With a map that shows the development of an area, you need to state how many phases of development there are. Then you need to identify when the most important or biggest development that happened. Finally describe the developments in more detail.

1 Read the exam question and look at the map. Then answer the questions.

    1 What type of map can you see: is it type 1 or type 2?
    2 What is planned for the town of Stanford?
    3 What does the flight path of the first site (A1) cross?
    4 Where is the runway of the second site (A2)?

The map below is of the town of Stanford and the surrounding area. A new airport (A) is planned for the town. The map shows two possible sites for the airport.

Summarize the information by selecting and reporting the main features and make comparisons where relevant.

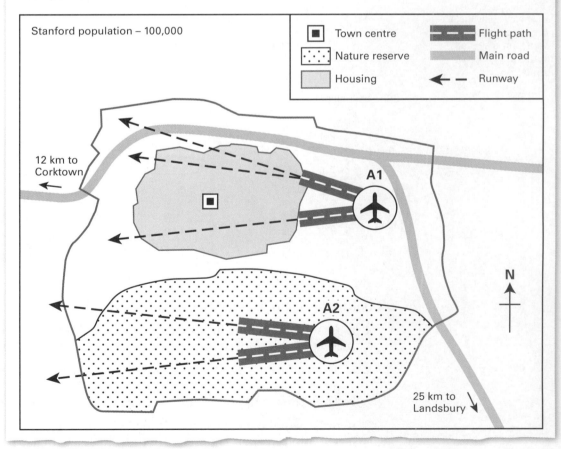

2 Read a sample answer to the exam question written by a student. Does the student follow the advice on page 48?

> The map shows two possible locations for a new airport near the town of Stanford.
>
> The main difference between the locations is that one would be near the town of Stanford and the other would be in the nature reserve close to the town.
>
> The location of the first site (A1) means that the flight paths of the aeroplanes would cross over areas of housing on the outskirts of the town. This may disturb residents of the town, which is a shame. In contrast, the flight path of the aeroplanes from the second site (A2) crosses over the nature reserve. This would disturb fewer people, but it may affect animals living in the reserve. The runways of the second site would be built in the nature reserve, which would mean that some trees would need to be cut down, causing terrible environmental damage, whereas the runways of the first site are outside the town. Luckily, it wouldn't be necessary to knock down any houses to build the airport. However, the closeness of the airport to the town might be dangerous if an aeroplane crashes. The first site is closer to main roads than the second site, making the first site easier to reach for tourists.
>
> Overall, both sites have disadvantages. For safety reasons, the site in the nature reserve would probably be better for the people of Stanford. And after all, people are more important than animals.

3 When you describe a map, it's not necessary to include comments which express your opinion. Delete the information in the student's answer which isn't necessary.

Skills practice

> The diagrams below show the stages and equipment used in the liquorice making process. Summarize the information by selecting and reporting the main features. Make comparisons where relevant.

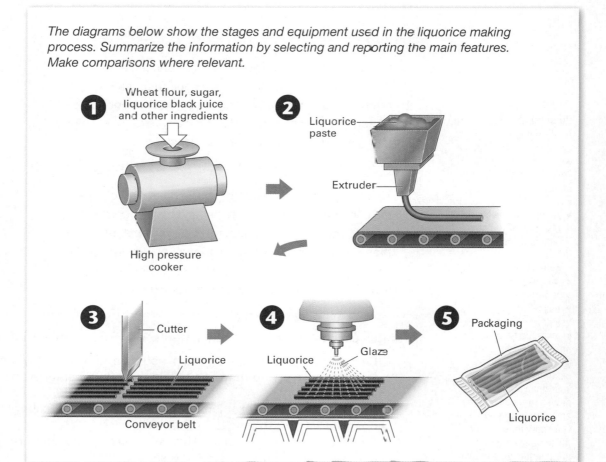

Analyzing the question and identifying the essay type

1 Read essay questions **A–D** below. Which IELTS subjects **1–9** do they relate to? Some questions may relate to more than one subject.

1 Technology	6 Media and entertainment
2 Family and upbringing	7 Success and happiness
3 Health and obesity	8 Art and creativity
4 Work	9 Transport
5 Education	

2 Look at the student's notes for topic A. Then underline key information in topics B, C and D and make notes.

'i.e use more often – don't use cars'.

'examples: bus, train, tram'.

'= rising every year → pollution'.

'= but – a contrast'

'causes: rising cost of public transport? Poor service? Inconvenience?'

'environmental damage'

A Governments around the world encourage people to make better use of public transport, yet the number of cars on the roads is increasing annually. **Discuss possible causes for this increase. What will the effects be?** Give reasons for your answer and include any relevant examples from your own knowledge or experience.

B In some countries, the rising cost of attending university has caused a lot of young people to consider alternative routes to employment. **To what extent do you think this is a positive or negative development?** Give reasons for your answer and include any relevant examples from your own knowledge or experience.

C In many countries the age that people can retire is increasing, making people work longer. **Discuss the advantages and disadvantages of this situation.** Give reasons for your answer and include any relevant examples from your own knowledge or experience.

D These days, children tend to spend a great deal of time on the computer, surfing the Internet and playing computer games. This can result in behavioural problems. **What are these problems and what solutions can you suggest?** Give reasons for your answer and include any relevant examples from your own knowledge or experience.

3 Match each instruction in bold in notes **A–D** to an explanation **1–4**.

1 I need to suggest the cause of a problem, and results it will have in the future.
2 I need to give my opinion in a balanced way, considering both sides of an argument.
3 I need to define the problem, give more details and examples and suggest possible ways of solving the problem.
4 I need to give my opinion on this issue, saying whether I think it's a good or a bad thing or whether I agree or disagree.

Remember

Analyze the question and think carefully about what it asks you to do. Try to recognize the type of essay you have to write. Is it:
- An opinion essay: Do I have to argue one side of the argument only, or do I have to give a balanced view?
- A cause–result essay
- A problem–solution essay?

You don't need special knowledge to answer an essay question but you do need to give examples to support your main points. Read newspapers as much as possible so that you know more about these topics and the arguments you can use.

Planning an essay

1 Read the essay question and the essay plans below. Which of the essay plans have these problems? Some essay plans may have more than one answer.

1 Only part of the essay question is answered.

2 The conclusion repeats the introduction.

3 The essay gives information that the essay question doesn't require.

2 Which essay plan do you think is most appropriate?

In many countries the age that people can retire is increasing, making people work longer.

Discuss the advantages and disadvantages of this situation.

Give reasons for your answer and include any relevant examples from your own knowledge or experience.

A

1 Introduction
  Increased retirement age in France and UK caused short & long-term problems
2 Disadvantages: short-term
  – Strikes e.g. teachers in UK
  – shorter retirement, more stress, health issues
3 Disadvantages: long-term
  – older workforce
  – fewer jobs for young people
4 Conclusion: summary of main ideas
  Solution-pay less into pensions?

$3+3=6+6=12$

B

Intro: retirement age increasing in France & UK etc. = unrest, strikes

Disadvantages: $0+1$

– shorter retirement, stress, health issues

– older workforce (more expensive)

– fewer jobs for young people

Advantages:

– working people more active, have a social life, earn money

– experienced, trained workforce

Conclusion: unavoidable, will have benefits

C

1 increased retirement age e.g. France and UK, has advantages and disadvantages:

2 Advantages
  – working people more active, have a social life, earn money
  – experienced, trained workforce

3 Disadvantages
  – shorter retirement, stress, health issues
  – older workforce (more expensive)
  – fewer jobs for young people

4 Conclusion: advantages and disadvantages to the increase in pension age.

Structuring the essay

1 Number paragraphs **A–D** in the correct order according to essay plan B above. Which parts are main points and which parts are examples? Which part introduces the next paragraph?

A One of these advantages is that experienced workers do not need as much training as younger workers. **An additional advantage** is that older people are forced to be active, which may result in better health into old age. Work **also** ensures that older people socialize and earn money, which allows them to lead independent lives.

B It seems **therefore**, that working longer has benefits for all: the older workers, companies and young employees. **Although** a later retirement age is an unpopular decision and it has disadvantages, it is perhaps necessary for a population who are living longer.

C One disadvantage is that people will have less time to enjoy life. **Consequently**, workers could suffer from health issues such as stress. **A further disadvantage of** an older workforce is that they may find it difficult to learn new skills, **such as** how to use new technology. **Also**, the more senior workers there are in a company, the fewer jobs there will be for young people. Older workers, **in addition**, cost companies more because they earn more. **However**, there are advantages to having more experienced workers in a company.

D The age of retirement in a number of countries around the world has been increased by the government. This is partly because people are living longer and **so** need to work for longer to have enough money when they retire. This has caused unrest in some countries. **For example**, in France and England there have been strikes. There are further disadvantages to an increased retirement age, **as well as** a number of advantages.

2 Match the words and phrases in bold in paragraphs **A–D** to categories **1–4**.

1 Additional ideas   **3** Contrast
2 Reasons/Consequence   **4** Examples

Remember
Use a variety of phrases and structures to make your writing more interesting to read. Use linking words and phrases to connect up your ideas.

3 Complete the sentences with the words from Exercise 2. Sometimes more than one answer is possible.

1 The age of retirement has increased. .... people work longer.
2 One disadvantage of a later retirement is the possible health problems it causes. .... is that older workers cost more money to employ.
3 Working longer means that older people can be independent. It .... means that they stay active for longer.
4 There are advantages to working longer. .... it is not popular.
5 Some companies benefit from an older workforce. ...., a company in Sweden uses its older employees to train younger staff.
6 Retiring later in life has benefits .... drawbacks.
7 Older workers may find it difficult to learn new skills .... IT skills.

Skills practice

1 Write an essay plan for question topic B on page 50.

2 Write the main body of the essay (not the introduction or the conclusion yet). Use the words and phrases in the box to help you.

> get into debt   take out a loan   get a low-paid job   be unemployed
> have no qualifications   on-the-job training   earn money   do manual work
> enter a profession   have good job prospects   gain work experience
> get an apprenticeship   academic qualifications   vocational qualifications

Writing a good introduction

1 Read the essay question and choose the introduction which follows the advice below.

> Governments around the world encourage people to make better use of public transport, yet the number of cars on the roads is increasing annually. Discuss possible causes for this increase. What will the effects be? Give reasons for your answer and include any relevant examples from your own knowledge or experience.

Good introductions should

1 summarize the topic without paraphrasing or repeating the question.
2 consider both sides of the question.
3 give an idea of the writer's position or opinion.
4 give an idea of how the essay will be structured.

> **A** Governments around the world encourage people to make better use of public transport, yet the number of cars on the roads is increasing annually. One possible reason for this is that public transport is expensive. This encourages people to use cars. In the long term, this will mean that governments will not provide public transport.

> **B** People are encouraged to use public transport rather than cars. However, the car is still a popular mode of transport. This has a number of serious consequences, both for public transport and for the environment. This essay will discuss the reasons why people prefer the car and will talk about the effects this choice has.

Using a range of language

1 Read introduction B above and find two synonyms (= words with a similar meaning) of words used in the exam question.

2 Paraphrasing helps you to use a variety of language in your essay, which makes your writing more interesting. Complete the paragraph with a word from the box.

comfortable	explanations	convenient	quiet

One reason that people might prefer the car is that it is more (1) .... than public transport. When you travel by car, you can go wherever you want at any time of day or night. There is no need to look at a timetable. Further (2) .... for the car's popularity is that it's (3) ...., private and more (4) .... You don't have to share your space with other people's noisy children and you always get a seat.

Remember
Read your essay after you have written it. Check that you have not repeated words and that you have used a variety of words to mean the same thing. Check your work for spelling, punctuation and grammar mistakes.

Being accurate

1 Look at the numbered words and the teacher's notes. Correct the mistakes.

Fewer people use ¹the buses and the trains so public ²transports companies increase ticket prices to ³do a **profit**. They also make more money by ⁴the **reduction** of the number of trains and buses and so provide a ⁵worst service than before. But **increased car use** ⁶have wider consequences. ⁷cars are more harmful to the environment than trains. One train ⁸who is filled with 100 people creates far less harmful greenhouse gas than one hundred cars.

---

1 article use *fewer people use buses and trains*

2 uncountable noun

3 verb combination: to .... a profit?

4 need a verb not a noun here

5 superlative or comparative here?

6 verb needs to 'agree' with subject

7 punctuation

8 relative clause. Use 'who' when a person is the subject.

Writing an effective conclusion

1 Read conclusions 1 and 2 below and choose which one you think is better. Use these questions to help you decide.
Which conclusion
  – sums up the essay question in different words?
  – identifies the most important cause of increased car use?
  – briefly sums up the effects of increased car use?

---

1 To conclude, people prefer to use their car instead of public transport because it is usually more convenient, quicker and more comfortable, and it is often cheaper. However, increased car use undoubtedly causes pollution and congestion. This is a problem which needs to be resolved in the future.

---

2 In conclusion, I think the reasons for people choosing to use the car are because it's more convenient than public transport and public transport isn't cheap or convenient. This choice has a lot of serious effects. Perhaps the government should pay for more environmentally friendly cars and encourage scientists to invent better fuel.

Skills practice

1 Look back at the essay plan that you wrote in response to the exam question below. Read the main body of the essay again. Write the introduction and conclusion of the essay.

In some countries, the rising cost of attending university has caused a lot of young people to consider alternative routes to employment. To what extent do you think this is a positive or negative development? Give reasons for your answer and include any relevant examples from your own knowledge or experience.

How much do you know about the IELTS Speaking module? Do the quiz below to find out.

Quiz

1 In the exam, you speak with
   A your partner   B an examiner
   C your teacher

2 The exam has three parts. Each part lasts for about .... minutes.
   A four   B ten   C two

3 Match the statements to the parts.
   1 You discuss your opinions about a subject.
   2 You answer questions about yourself and your life.
   3 You speak on your own for 1–2 minutes.
   4 You have time to plan your answer.
   5 You are given a card with a topic to talk about.
   6 The subject you talk about is connected to the subject in Part two.

   A Part 1
   B Part 2
   C Part 3

4 Which of these will gain a higher score in the exam? Complete the table.
   1 only talking about topics that are familiar to you e.g. your family
   2 linking sentences together with words like 'and', 'because' and 'so'
   3 making frequent grammatical mistakes
   4 pronouncing words correctly
   5 using a variety of vocabulary
   6 repeating the same word many times
   7 pausing a lot to think about the language you need
   8 replying to a question with a one word answer e.g. 'yes'

Higher score	Lower score

Part 1

Skills development

Getting started

Remember
Bring the correct form of identification with you to the speaking exam, for example, your passport or identification card. You <u>must</u> bring the same form of identification that you used on your application form.

1 At the beginning of Part 1, the examiner will check your identity by asking you questions. Choose the <u>best</u> answer for each of the questions below.

   1 Can you tell me your full name please?
      A Good morning. Yes, it's Andrea.
      B Yes, my name's Andrea Popovska.
      C Yes, it's Popovska.

   2 Can you tell me where you're from?
      A I'm coming from Russia but I'm living in London at the moment.
      B I'm originally from Moscow in Russia, but I live in London now.
      C Moscow, in Russia.

   3 Can I see your identification please?
      A Yes, sure, here you are.
      B Yes.
      C No, I'm sorry, I don't have any.

Learning key vocabulary

1 In Part 1 the examiner will ask you about yourself and about 'everyday' subjects. Complete the mind maps of subjects below with vocabulary from the box.

Useful language

busy   degree   delicious   eat out   facilities   fast food   graduation/graduate from
healthy food   historic   ~~main course~~   modern   population   qualification/qualify for
study   secondary school   subjects   suburbs/outskirts   ~~typical dishes~~

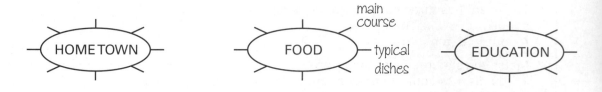

2 Add two more of your own words to each mind map. Then make mind maps for <u>three</u> of the subjects below.

1	Friends	**3**	Holidays	**5**	Family	**7**	Your country
2	Work	**4**	Leisure	**6**	Clothes	**8**	Favourite places

Answering the question

1 Match questions **1–11** with a topic from Exercises 1 and 2 above. Then complete each question with one word.

Question	Answer
1 .... did you last visit this place?	It was a long time ago, I think around 1992, when I was a little girl.
2 .... do you do?	I'd like to be a doctor in the future.
3 .... do you do to keep fit?	It depends on the weather. In the Summer, I go jogging, but in the Winter, I go to the gym.
4 .... often do you see your best friend?	We don't see each other very often because we live so far apart, so, about once or twice a year.
5 .... do you enjoy your job?	Because it's interesting.
6 .... you go out for an evening, ... do you like to do?	My favourite thing to do is to go to the cinema. My friends and I all like horror or science-fiction films.
7 .... fashion important to you?	No.
8 .... popular is this food in your country?	You could probably call pasta a national dish! Everyone eats it, more or less every day.
9 .... part of the town do you live in?	I live in the city centre, just off the High Street. It's very convenient, but can be noisy.
10 .... did you last go on holiday?	Barbados.
11 .... is your favourite school subject?	Well, I really enjoy studying Geography.

2 Which answer(s) do you think

    A is/are too short?
    B give(s) enough information?
    C doesn't/don't answer the question?
    D give(s) reasons for the answer?

Using the correct tense

1 Look at questions **1–3** and underline the verbs. Then choose the answer which best matches the verb form in the question.

    1 Has your country changed much since you were a child?
        A Definitely. It is very big with a lot of industry now.
        B Yes, of course. It was small and quiet when I was young.
        C Yes. It's grown from a small town to a much bigger place.

    2 Was it easy for you to get this qualification?
        A No, not really. I've worked hard for years.
        B Actually, it was quite difficult. I had to work full time and study at night.
        C No, it's quite a challenge as I don't like studying very much.

    3 What would you like to do in the future?
        A I try to live in the present and not think about the future.
        B I applied for a job at a law firm last week because lawyers are well paid.
        C I'd like to study to become a teacher and perhaps have children one day.

> **Remember**
> When the examiner asks a question, listen to the verb form in the question and try to use the same verb form in your answer. Then, when you continue to give more detail in the rest of your answer, you can use different tenses.
> e.g. Where would you like to go for your next holiday?
> *I'd like to go to Italy. I'd particularly like to visit Rome because I've never been there before and I've heard that it's beautiful. Last year we went to Puglia in the South of Italy …*

2 It's better to use more than one tense in your answer. It shows you can use lots of different grammar structures. Underline the verbs in the answer below and say what tenses the candidate uses (e.g. present simple, past simple etc).

Examiner: *Tell me about your home town.*

Candidate: *I live on the outskirts of a small, historic town in south-east Germany. Um, I've lived there for twenty three years. The town has changed quite a lot in this time. It used to be much smaller but a few years ago, a car manufacturer opened on the outskirts and this encouraged a lot of people to move to the town to look for jobs.*

3 Choose the correct tense to complete this answer. Sometimes both tenses are possible.

Examiner: *Tell me about your best friend.*

Candidate: *Her name is Frida.* **I've known** / **I knew** *her since we* **were** / **have been** *both at school. The funny thing is that at first we* **didn't** / **don't** *like each other, but one day I* **shout** / **shouted** *at a girl who* **was** / **has been** *horrible to Frida and we* **became** / **become** *friends. We* **see** / **saw** *each other about once a month and we always* **have** / **had** *a great time.* **I'm going to see** / **I'm seeing** *her next week for a very special occasion – she's getting married.*

Speaking fluently

1 Read the answer below and choose the correct question **A–C**.

    A What's your favourite hobby?
    B What's your favourite photograph?
    C Why do you like photographs?

    Well, I think it's probably taking photographs. Usually I take my camera with me when I go out, and sometimes I'm lucky and see something which makes a wonderful photo. At other times, I'm not so lucky. I used to go to photography classes but now I don't have enough money to do that and anyway, I prefer to teach myself. I love photography because it's a way of keeping a moment in time forever.

2 Find four adverbs of time and frequency in the answer, e.g. *usually.*

3 Look at the words in bold below and match sentence beginnings **A–C** to endings **1–3**. Then answer the questions below the table.

A	I like playing golf	**1**	and **anyway**, it's too expensive.
B	I don't have time to go to an evening class	**2**	**but** I hate taking him out in the rain.
C	I usually enjoy walking my dog	**3**	**because** it's a good form of exercise and you get lots of fresh air.

In the sentence endings, which word in bold

1 introduces a contrast?
2 introduces a second idea that supports the first?
3 introduces a reason?

4 Complete the answer to the question below with words from Exercises 2 and 3 above.

Examiner: *How popular is football in your country?*

Candidate: *Well, you could call it a national sport. Matches are (1) ....
on a Sunday and whole families go to watch. I really enjoy watching football
(2) .... the players are really skilful. It's like an art. I used to play
(3) .... I had to stop (4) .... I hurt my knee, and
(5) ...., I wasn't very good at it. My brother still plays though and
(6) ...., when I'm not busy, I go to watch his matches. He's a much better
player than me.*

Skills practice

1 🔘**21** Listen to two candidates, A and B, answering a question, and read the recording script on page 93. Which candidate do you think gives the best answer? Why? Think about the following questions.
Which candidate

1 doesn't hesitate too much?
2 uses a better range of vocabulary?
3 uses grammar accurately?
4 answers all parts of the question fully?
5 has pronunciation which is easier to understand?
6 uses connecting words, linkers and adverbs of frequency?

2 Look again at the 'everyday' subjects on page 56. Choose three topics and write four questions that an examiner might ask for each topic.

3 Practise answering the questions and record your answers if possible. Then listen to your recording and complete this checklist.

- Did you give enough information?
- Did you give reasons for your answer?
- Did you use the appropriate tenses?
- Did you use linking words and discourse markers?
- Did you use a range of vocabulary?

Part 2

Skills development

Planning your answer: writing notes

1 In Part 2 of the Speaking module, you are given a card with a question on it. You will have one minute to read the question and make notes on your answer. Look at two students' notes for the question below. Which notes do you think would be more useful in an exam?

Describe your favourite place. You should say:

- where it is

- when you first went there

- what it looks like

and explain why you like it.

A It's in Croatia on the Dalmatian Coast, it's a city called Dubrovnik. When I was very little, with my family, but went back again last year. It's a walled city and it's unusual because it's surrounded by sea. It's really beautiful.

B Croatia, Dubrovnik
Child, with family. Last year.
Walled, unusual location, beautiful

Introducing ideas and opinions

You can prepare for Part 2 of the Speaking module by learning useful phrases to introduce your ideas and opinions.

These useful phrases often begin with words that link to the question, or to the sentences before. Some useful phrases are:

What I like about ... is that ...
The good / interesting / best thing about ... is that
The reason that I like ... is that ...
The place / person / thing I like / admire the most is ...
The place where I first saw ... was ...

e.g. **What** I like about running, **is** that it isn't competitive.
The best thing about running, **is** that it's not competitive.
The reason I don't like football, is that it's boring to watch.
The person (who) I admire the most, is my sister.
The place where I first saw David was Florence, in Italy.

1 ⊙22 Listen to a student's answer to the exam question on page 59 and tick the phrase (a or b) that you hear.

  1 a One of my favourite places is in Croatia.
    b Croatia is one of my favourite places.

  2 a I like Dubrovnik because of its location.
    b What I like about Dubrovnik is its location.

  3 a You can combine a city break with swimming and sunbathing, which is good.
    b The good thing about this is that you can combine a city break with lots of swimming and sunbathing.

2 Complete the sentences with answers which are true for you. Use the prompts in brackets to help you.

   a The reason I don't like .... (a place) is that

   ....

   b The interesting thing about .... (a person) is that

   he/she is ....

   c What I admire about .... (a person) is that he/she is

   ....

   d The good thing about .... (an activity) is that it's

   ....

3 Read the exam question and the student's notes. Use the notes to answer the question. Try to use the useful phrases for introducing ideas.

> Describe a restaurant that you enjoyed going to.
>
> You should say:
>
> - where the restaurant was
>
> - why you chose this restaurant
>
> - what type of food you ate in this restaurant
>
> and explain why you enjoyed eating in this restaurant.

> –'Effi's' in Istanbul, Turkey
> – birthday party, recommended by hotel
> – Turkish food: kebabs, meze, pilav
> – great atmosphere, food delicious

Organizing your answer

1 ⊙ 23 Listen to a student's answer to the question 'Describe a piece of art you like' and number the parts of the question in the order that the student answers them.

   A who made it
   B where you first saw it
   C what the piece of art is
   D why you like it

2 ⊙ 23 Complete sentences **A–D** with one word. Then listen again and check your answers.

   A .... of my favourite art works is called ...
   B The .... where I first saw *David* was in ...
   C An .... called Michelangelo created the sculpture ...
   D The .... I like the statue is that ...

3 Read the exam question in Exercise 5. How does the student introduce each point of the question?

   A He repeats the points on the card using the same words.
   B He uses different words to talk about the points on the card.

4 The student adds extra detail which is not included in the question. Read the answer in the recording script on p93 and underline the extra detail.

5 Read the question and a student's answer below. Use the phrases in Exercise 2 above to improve the student's answer. Then add extra detail from the box below.

Describe a piece of art you like. You should say:

- what the piece of art is and who made it
- what it looks like
- where you first saw it

and explain why you like it.

What is the piece of art? It's called 'Composition VIII'. The kind of art is a painting. It's abstract. A artist called Wassily Kadinsky painted it. I first saw it in a gallery in New York when I was a music student. I like it because it is different. Kadinsky thought that art was like music. He said that 'the soul is the piano with many strings'.

oil painting   painted in 1923   Russian artist
Guggenheim museum, New York
Painting full of shapes – circles, semi-circles, triangles   Lots of lines   two dimensional

Using stress and intonation

1 ⊙**24** Listen to two examples of the same answer. Which example A or B sounds more interesting?

2 ⊙**24** Listen to example B again. Underline words in the first two lines which are 'stressed' (emphasized by being said more loudly or with greater force).

The person I admire the most is my mother. The reason I think she's wonderful is that she has always put her children first.

3 It's important to vary the tone of your voice so that you sound more interesting. Read and listen to these sentences. Then listen again and repeat them. Copy the intonation used.

The PERSON I admire the MOST Is my MOther.

The REASON I think she's WONDERFUL is that she has ALWAYS put her CHILDREN FIRST.

Remember
After you finish answering the question on your card, the examiner will often ask you some more questions. Try to answer them in complete sentences and give more details where possible.

Skills practice

1 Read the question and make notes. Stop after one minute.

Describe an interesting historic place in your country. You should say:

- what the place is
- where the place is
- what you can see there now

and explain why the place is interesting.

2 Practise answering the question. Then practise with another student. Complete this checklist for your partner and ask them to complete their checklist for you.

> - Did you give enough information?
> - Did you give reasons for your answer?
> - Did you use the appropriate tenses?
> - Did you link your ideas together?
> - Did you use focusing phrases to introduce your ideas?
> - Did you answer all the parts of the question?
> - Did you use synonyms and organize your answer correctly?
> - Did your answer sound interesting?

Part 3

Remember
In Part 3 of the exam, the examiner asks you further questions which are connected to the topic of the question in Part 2.
These questions encourage you to talk about less personal, more abstract ideas and topics.

Skills development

Discussing topics

1 Which question(s) (**A–F**) is asking the speaker to

   1 consider both sides of an argument?
   2 make suggestions and give examples?
   3 make a prediction?

   A Do you think the Internet is a good or a bad thing?
   B What are the advantages and disadvantages of learning a foreign language?
   C Do you think people will have more or less free time in the future?
   D What kinds of things do you think students should learn in history lessons?
   E What do you think the consequences of increasing fuel prices will be?
   F Which is better: having a lot of money or having close friends?

2 ⊙25 Listen and say which three of the questions **A–F** above the students answer.

3 ⊙25 Listen again to the first answer and number expressions **A–D** in the order that you hear them.

   A whereas   **C** Overall though, I think …
   B In my opinion …   **D** Unfortunately …

4 Listen again to the second answer and match expressions **A–E** with the correct sentence ending.

A	I don't think that …	**1**	money can actually make you lonely.
B	I believe that …	**2**	stay with you whether you are rich or poor.
C	It seems that …	**3**	to have good friends than money.
D	Real friends, on the other hand …	**4**	money can buy you happiness.
E	It's much better …	**5**	it's much more important to have good friends than to be rich.

Remember
Part 3 is a discussion with the examiner. Listen carefully to the examiner's questions and answer each question as fully as possible, so that the examiner can listen and get a good idea of your language level.
Include extra detail in your answer but make sure you answer the question – don't include information which isn't relevant.

5 Read phrases **A–D** and decide whether they introduce positive, negative or neutral information. Then listen and check your answers.

   A I hope that …   **C** However, I'm afraid that …
   B Fortunately …   **D** Realistically …

Skills practice

1 Choose three of the questions **A–F** above and practise answering them. Then find a friend to be the 'examiner'. Ask them to complete the checklist at the top of the page. Did you use language to express your opinion?

Listening

Section 1   Questions 1–10

Questions 1–5

⊙26 Complete the notes below. Write **NO MORE THAN ONE WORD AND/OR A NUMBER** for each answer.

Details of the car

Age / mileage: about (1) .... years old and has done approx. 40,000 miles.

History: had (2) .... previous owners.

Reason for sale: selling it because has a (3) .... in London – no car needed.

Final price: agreed (4) £.........................

Appointment: offered to meet on Saturday, at (5) .... a.m., in the café.

Questions 6–10

⊙27 Complete the form below. Write **NO MORE THAN TWO WORDS AND/OR A NUMBER** for each answer.

WAYNE'S WHEELS INSURANCE

APPLICATION FORM

Name:	Mohammed (6) ....
Date of birth:	21st (7) ....
Car make:	Peugeot (8) ....
Registration number:	(9) ....
Address:	78 Acacia Avenue, Stourbridge, Wolverhampton, BM56 YLM
Total annual insurance (incl. admin charge):	(10) £.........................

Section 2   Questions 11–20

Questions 11 and 12

⊙28 Choose the correct letter, **A, B** or **C.**

11 All the students on the course
   A are native English speakers.
   B are from Asian countries.
   C have jobs in law.

12 The blended learning course is
   A taught face-to-face for half of the year.
   B taught online with two face-to-face meetings.
   C taught completely online with virtual exams.

Questions 13–17

🔘 28 Complete the flow chart. Write **NO MORE THAN TWO WORDS AND/OR A NUMBER** for each answer.

How to use the virtual learning platform (VLP)

> Log-on to the platform. Download the first (13) .... and ....

> Buy books on (14) .... or download them from VLP

> If you need help, contact tutor by (15) ...., or phone.

> If you prefer, ask students for help via the (16) ....

> Get (17) .... from tutor on VLP a week later.

Questions 18–20

Choose **THREE** letters **A–F**.

What **THREE** things can you do on the blended learning course?

A participate in seminars at any time
B meet with your tutor at regular times
C listen to lectures at a time of your choice
D study on a full-time basis at a distance
E have more time to finish an assignment
F have another year to complete your degree

Section 3   Questions 21–30

Questions 21–26

🔘 29 Complete the sentences below. Write **NO MORE THAN ONE WORD** for each answer.

21 The tutor is pleased that Jane is always well .... for seminars.
22 Jane enjoys the psychology seminars and is good at ....
23 The lecture on critical thinking was about asking particular types of ....
24 Jane should think about the .... supporting other students' theories.
25 The tutor is .... that Jane makes claims which are not proved.
26 Jane needs to use more .... as evidence for claims she makes.

Questions 27–30

What are the disadvantages of each type of research?

Choose your answers from **A–F** below and write the letters next to questions **27–30**.

27 Case studies ....
28 Research papers ....
29 Interviews ....
30 Questionnaires ....

A don't give very detailed information.
B can encourage a particular answer.
C don't provide enough information.
D may make a theory or argument weaker.
E can produce very unscientific results.
F can be out-of-date.

Section 4   Questions 31–40

Questions 31–35

⊙**30** Complete the table below. Write **NO MORE THAN TWO WORDS AND/OR A NUMBER** for each answer.

The Great Pyramid of Khufu	
Reason for interest	Because of the (31) .... and size of the pyramid
(32)	5.9 million tons
Height	(33) .... metres tall
Materials	(34) .... stone blocks
Date	2550 BC: took (35) .... to complete
Number of workers	20,000–30,000
Mystery	How could workers move a stone block weighing two tons?

Questions 36–40

Complete the diagrams. Write **NO MORE THAN ONE WORD AND/OR A NUMBER** for each answer.

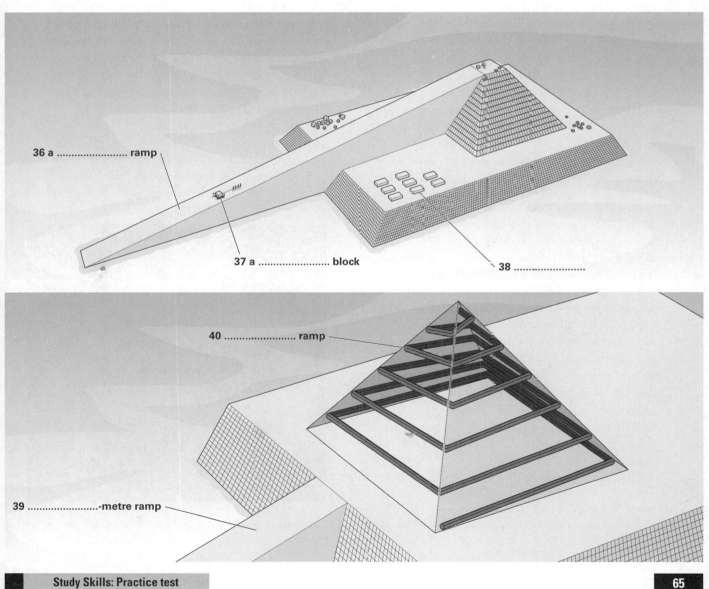

36 a .... ramp

37 a .... block

38 ....

40 .... ramp

39 ....-metre ramp

Reading

Reading Passage 1

You should spend about 20 minutes on questions **1–13**, which are based on Reading Passage 1 below.

Telescope to detect ET on his mobile

A Astronomers are planning to build the world's largest telescope – a machine so powerful it could detect radio signals from a planet up to 50 light years, or 13.5 billion years from Earth. The giant radio-telescope is called the Square Kilometre Array (SKA) and will consist of 3,000 separate radio dishes and other antennae all linked together into one huge machine. It will generate 100 times more data than all the information currently on the Internet and will need the world's most powerful supercomputer to analyze the information it collects.

B The SKA will work in a similar way to other large radio telescopes such as Australia's CSIRO Parkes radio telescope, also known as 'The Dish'. The telescope gets its name from the bowl-shaped reflector called a 'dish' that is used to collect radio waves from space. The reflector focuses the waves onto an antenna that changes them into electric signals. From the antenna, the signals are transmitted down into the control room at the base of the telescope and are picked up by a radio receiver. This receiver makes the signals stronger. The signals are then analyzed by a computer at another location and the information is used to draw a picture of the source of the radio waves.

C Compared to 'The Dish', however, SKA will be thousands of times more sensitive. This sensitivity is because of its size; the larger the dish, or the more dishes there are, the more powerful the radio signal can be, allowing unknown areas of the universe to be discovered. 'We know that the universe is incredibly vast, containing hundreds of billions of stars,' said Richard Schilizzi, director of the SKA project. 'However, at present we can only see a fraction of what is out there. The SKA will enable us to explore some of its furthest reaches.' Scientists hope to find alien life intelligent enough to invent radio. The SKA will be able to detect a mobile phone system within 50 light years of Earth, but will also probably be able to scan star systems which are much further away, because any advanced life form would have powerful radio emitters such as radar and radio stations.

D But looking for evidence of extraterrestrial life is just one of many tasks for the SKA. Scientists also hope that the telescope will help them to understand how the first stars and planets were formed, during a period of time called 'first light'. 'The SKA is a bit like a time machine,' said Phil Diamond, head of the astronomy and space science division of CSIRO, the Australian government's research arm. 'It will gather radiation emitted more than 13 billion years ago, allowing us to get a picture of what the universe looked like then. By choosing the type of radiation we look at, we can get similar pictures of the universe from any other era we choose – so we can watch how it evolved.'

E More than 20 countries will share the estimated £1.4 billion cost of the project for the telescope. Two potential sites have been chosen, one in Western Australia and the other in South Africa. Both are in the southern hemisphere because this will give the instrument a direct line of sight into the heart of the Milky Way. The SKA must be built on a site completely free of radio interference – with the host country promising it will prevent the construction of any mobile phone, radio or TV masts for up to 50 years. This means it will have to be built mainly in a desert – either in the outback of Western Australia or the Karoo of South Africa.

Questions 1–4

Reading Passage 1 has five paragraphs, **A–E**.

Choose the correct heading for paragraphs **B–E** from the list of headings below.

> **List of headings**
> **i** Budgeting for the construction of SKA
> **ii** Discovering the secret origins of our universe
> **iii** Abilities of advanced life forms
> **iv** Potential to see further than before
> **v** Methods of mapping the location of the planets
> **vi** Plans for the world's largest telescope
> **vii** Location considerations for SKA
> **viii** The collection and analysis of radio waves

Example   *Answer*
Paragraph A   vi

Questions 5–8

The diagram below shows how a large radio telescope works.

Label the diagram. Choose **NO MORE THAN TWO WORDS** from the passage for each answer.

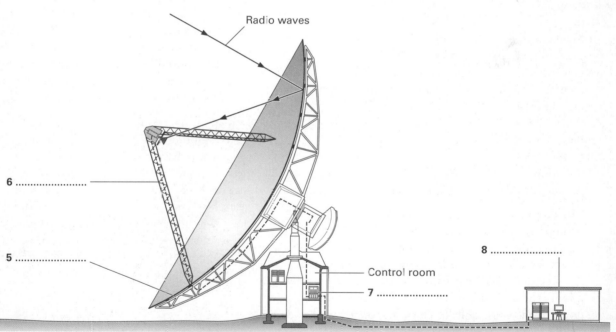

Radio waves

6 ....

5 ....

Control room

7 ....

8 ....

Questions 9–13

Do the following statements agree with the information given in Reading Passage 1?

Write:

TRUE   if the statement agrees with the information
FALSE   if the statement contradicts the information
NOT GIVEN   if there's no information on this

9   The SKA will be made from many parts.
10   The SKA will be the world's most powerful telescope.
11   About one third of the universe has been discovered.
12   Scientists hope to get in touch with aliens by mobile phone.
13   Governments have decided where the SKA will be built.

Reading

Reading Passage 2

You should spend about 20 minutes on questions **14–26**, which are based on Reading Passage 2 below.

The Real Price of Gold

Like many of his Inca ancestors, Juan Apaza spends every day digging for gold. For 30 days each month Apaza works, without pay, deep inside a mine above the world's highest town, La Rinconada. For 30 days he faces terrible dangers – explosions, poisonous gases, tunnel collapses – to find the gold that the world demands. Apaza does all this, without pay, so that he can spend the 31st day of the month taking as much rock as he can carry from the mine for himself. This rock may contain a lot of gold which could make Apaza a very wealthy man, but it may be completely worthless. But unbelievably, Apaza and his fellow miners want to take that risk. 'It's a cruel lottery,' says Apaza. 'But at least it gives us hope.'

For more than 500 years the dream of gold has attracted people to this place in Peru. The first were the Inca, then the Spanish, whose search for gold and silver led them to take over the New World. But it is only now, as the price of gold increases dramatically – it has risen 235 percent in the past eight years – that 30,000 people have come to La Rinconada, turning this once quiet village into a horribly polluted town on top of the world. La Rinconada is not a pleasant place to live in or to visit. During my time here, I feared for my health and safety. La Rinconada has few basic services: no piped water, no pollution control, no postal service, not even a police station. It's a dangerous place, where no law is respected.

The dirt and rubbish on the overcrowded streets are small problems compared with the tons of poisonous mercury released during the process of separating gold from rock. According to Peruvian environmentalists, the mercury released at La Rinconada and the nearby mining town of Ananea is poisoning rivers and lakes down to the coast of Lake Titicaca, more than a hundred miles away.

Admittedly, gold mines do have a few advantages: they can bring jobs, technologies, and development to poor areas. Gold mining, however, wastes more energy per ounce than any other metal. To mine a single ounce of gold – the amount in a typical wedding ring – requires the removal of more than 250 tons of rock. Yet the public continue to buy it even though the price of gold is rising dramatically. Jewellery shops are, without doubt, partly to blame. They are responsible for two-thirds of the demand for gold, and made $53.5 billion in worldwide sales last year. Disappointingly, the origin of the gold and the damage caused by gold mining doesn't seem to concern them. Despite action groups trying to stop jewellery shops from selling gold from mines that cause serious damage, many countries which rely on the sale of gold to help the economy ignore the protests.

In many ways, people are interested in gold because there's not much of it. In all of history, only 161,000 tons of gold have been mined, only just enough to fill two Olympic-size swimming pools. More than half of that has been taken out of the ground in the past 50 years. Now the world's supplies of gold are quickly going down and new discoveries are rare. Most of the gold left is underground in far-off places which are often beauty spots. It's only a matter of time before these are discovered by the mining companies.

Questions 14–17

Choose the correct letter, **A**, **B**, **C** or **D**

14 Apaza works in the gold mine because
    A he needs a full-time job.
    B he earns a lot of money at the end of the month.
    C he could become very rich one day.
    D his family have always worked in a mine.

15 The most serious problem described in La Rinconada is
    A the increase in the price of gold.
    B the over-crowded gold mining villages.
    C the poison released into the water.
    D the lack of facilities in La Rinconada.

16 Gold mining causes
    A poverty and unemployment.
    B energy to be wasted.
    C the price of gold to increase.
    D action groups to blame jewellers.

17 There is a shortage of gold because
    A the gold is in protected areas.
    B people haven't discovered where it is yet.
    C a lot of it has been mined already.
    D the gold is difficult to reach.

Questions 18–21

Do the following statements agree with the writer's opinion given in Reading Passage 2?
Write:

YES   if the statement agrees with the opinion of the writer
NO   if the statement contradicts the opinion of the writer
NOT GIVEN   if it's impossible to say what the writer thinks about this

18 The benefits of gold mining are greater than the drawbacks.
19 La Riconada is not a pleasant place to live.
20 Jewellery shops shouldn't sell gold.
21 Nature should be protected from miners.

Questions 22–26

Complete the summary using the list of words, **A–E** below.

Gold mining is a very (22) .... and dirty business, both for the miners and
for the (23) .... Unfortunately, it's also very profitable. As the supply of gold
has decreased, the price of it has gone up, resulting in a higher demand for gold than
ever before. (24) .... in particular, are responsible for the increased demand.
Although mining does create (25) .... it also creates a lot of waste and
(26) .... which damages towns, water supplies and areas of natural beauty.

  A jewellers
  B employers
  C dangerous
  D miners' families
  E risk
  F improvements
  G environment
  H jobs
  I pollution

You should spend about 20 minutes on questions **27–40**, which are based on Reading Passage 3 below.

History of Silk Production

Silk from the moth, *Bombyx mori* (L.), has a long and colourful history unknown to most people. Silk production was discovered in 2,700 BC, almost 5,000 years ago. Chinese legend tells the story of Si Ling Chi, a Chinese princess, who sat in the shade of her court garden, sipping tea beneath mulberry trees. She heard a tiny noise in the leaves above her, and a white cocoon dropped into her teacup. Instead of picking it out of her drink, she watched as the hot water began to dissolve it. Soon her tea was full of shining silk threads and Si Ling Chi imagined the beautiful clothes she might create for her husband.

Si Ling Chi went on to develop sericulture, the science of silk production. She learned to keep silk worms, to collect the silk fibres, to test them for strength, and how to weave them into clothes. Si Ling Chi was later honoured with the name *Seine-Than*, or 'The Goddess of Silk Worms'. Sericulture during the following centuries spread through China and soon became a state secret. It remained a mystery to other countries for thousands of years. In 139 BC, the world's longest highway was opened, from eastern China to the Mediterranean Sea. One of the most valuable commodities to travel along the road was silk and for this reason, the road was named 'Silk Road'. By the middle of the first century AD, people in Rome were becoming frustrated that they could not learn the secrets of the valuable material but the Chinese kept the secrets of sericulture so safe that the early Romans never learned it.

The Chinese finally lost their secret to India. According to legend, the egg of the silk moth and the seed of the mulberry tree were carried to India hidden in the headdress of a Chinese princess. From India the silk industry spread into Persia and Central Asia. The emperor Justinian gained the secrets of sericulture for the Roman Empire in 522 AD, when Persian monks brought the eggs into the country illegally. In 877 AD, the soldier Biachu captured Canfu, the centre of foreign silk trade in China, destroyed all of the mulberry trees and silkworms of the region, and put high taxes on all foreign trade. These actions stopped China exporting silk and other goods for more than 60 years. However, by this time, silk production was practised in Western Asia and Eastern Europe and the price of silk around the world remained the same. During the 18th and 19th centuries, Europeans also made important progress in silk production. England improved silk-weaving techniques and roller printing. In 1801, A Frenchman named Joseph Jacquard exhibited his new machine for silk weaving and this gradually spread through the industry. These advances introduced a more mechanized and scientific approach to silk production than existed previously.

Sericulture has also been attempted in the United States, but has been largely unsuccessful Hoping to make a lot of money, thousands of individuals bought mulberry plants and planted large areas of valuable land. The money they spent was more than the money that was made, and bad weather destroyed the plants. In the course of a few years, many failures and great disappointments caused the USA to almost give up sericulture. Although there were several more attempts at sericulture in California from the 1860's through the early 1900's and some silk was produced during this time, most attempts failed and sericulture never became permanently established in the state.

Silk production today is a mix of the ancient and the modern. The first stage of silk production is hatching the silkworm eggs. Larvae are then fed cut-up mulberry leaves and after a period of time they spin their silken cocoons. The silk thread comes from the head of each larva and is stuck together with a sticky substance called sericin. Cocoons are later washed in hot water to remove the sericin, which frees the silk threads. Single threads are then combined to form yarn. This yarn is eventually wound onto reels. The yarn is dried, packed according to quality, and is now ready for sale.

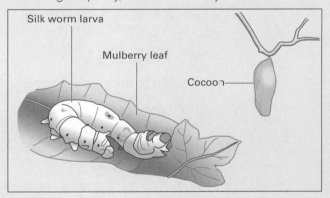

Silk worm larva

Mulberry leaf

Cocoon

World silk production has approximately doubled during the last 30 years in spite of the competition from man-made fibre. China during this period has been responsible for over 50% of the world production of silk each year. Consequently, the country that first developed sericulture approximately 4,700 years ago has again become the world's main producer of silk.

Questions 27–31

Match each event with the correct nationality **A–H**

- A Chinese
- B Romans
- C Indians
- D Persians
- E Europeans
- F Americans

27 invested money in silk production
28 learned about silk illegally
29 made silk production mechanical
30 make half of the world's silk
31 were the first, after the Chinese, to learn about silk

Questions 32–35

Choose **FOUR** letters **A–F**.

Which **FOUR** of the following statements are true of silk?

- A It is a entirely man-made fibre these days.
- B Its production was discovered by accident.
- C Its production was modernized in the 18th century.
- D It was more successful in the past than now.
- E Its production is a combination of old and new methods.
- F Its production reached Europe from Persia.

Questions 36–40

Complete the flow chart.

Write **NO MORE THAN ONE WORD** from the passage for each answer.

Process of silk production

Hatching
Silkworm (36) .... hatched.

Feeding
Larvae fed (37) .... from the mulberry tree.

Spinning
Larvae produce thread from (38) ....

Washing
(39) .... washed to separate silk threads.

Packaging
Silk (40) .... created and packaged for sale.

Writing Task 1

You should spend about 20 minutes on this task.

The graphs below show the number of international tourists by month and by year, and which regions of the world they visit. Summarize the information by selecting and reporting the main features and make comparisons where relevant.

Write at least 150 words.

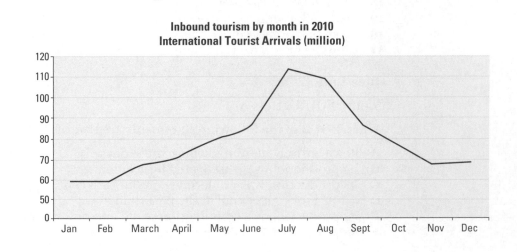

Inbound tourism by month in 2010
International Tourist Arrivals (million)

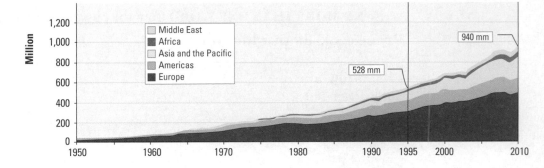

International Tourist Arrivals by region (million)

Writing Task 2

You should spend about 40 minutes on this task.

Write about the following topic:

Air travel produces 3–5% of the carbon dioxide released into the atmosphere, and is predicted to become the world's largest cause of environmental damage and global warming. Governments around the world plan to increase the cost of flying to encourage people to fly less. To what extent do you agree with the governments' plans?

Give reasons for your answer and include any relevant examples from your own knowledge or experience.

Write at least 250 words.

Part 1

The examiner asks you some general questions about yourself, your home, your job or your studies. For example:

Tell me about your country.

What do you do in your spare time?

How important is your family to you?

What are your plans for the future?

Part 2

The examiner gives you a card with questions on a topic. You will have one minute to think about the topic and plan what you're going to say. You can make notes if you wish. You should then talk about the topic for one to two minutes.

> Describe something you own which is very important to you.
> You should say:
>
> - where you got it from
> - how long you have had it
> - what you use it for
>
> and explain why it is important to you.

Part 3

The examiner asks you further questions which are connected to the topic of Part 2. These questions give you the opportunity to discuss more abstract issues and ideas.

Example questions:

Let's talk a bit more about possessions ...

What's more important, possessions or experiences?

What sort of possessions give people status in your country?

What object do most young people want to own?

Finally, let's talk about the role of advertising ...

Do you think that advertising influences what people buy?

Answer key

Key for Listening module

Quiz p. 7

1 A The listening test lasts for about 40 minutes.
2 B There are 40 questions and 40 points.
3 B You will hear each part of the listening once.
4 True. You also have time after the listening to check your answers.
5 True. You will have ten minutes at the end of the listening to transfer your answers onto the answer sheet.
6 A Two people talking. Their topic of conversation could be about an aspect of student life.
7 B One person talking. In the second section, this could be a presentation on something related to study, though it won't be about an academic subject. In the fourth section, the presentation will relate to an academic subject, but you won't need specialist knowledge to understand it.
8 C Up to four people talking. This could be a seminar discussion or a discussion between students and a tutor. The topic of discussion is academic but you won't need specialist subject knowledge to understand it.
9 A and C The listening module gets progressively more difficult so Sections 3 and 4 are more difficult than Sections 1 and 2.
10 False. You don't need to have specialist subject knowledge to do well in the exam.

Completing a form: predicting topic vocabulary p. 7

1 3 Accommodation form. Possible key words: bedrooms, location
2 1 Minguez. 'Yes, it's <u>Minguez</u>.' 'OK, is that M-I-N-G-E-Z?' 'No, it's <u>M-I-N-G-U-E-Z</u>.'
   2 C.J. 'OK, thank you. And your first name?' 'It's Carlos-Jerez'. 'Hmm, so that's initials <u>C. J.</u>' 'Yes.'
   3 single. 'And are you married Carlos?' 'No, I'm not.'
   4 student. 'OK What do you do for a living Carlos?' 'Sorry, I don't understand.' 'What's your job?' 'Oh, I don't have a job. I'm <u>studying at university</u> at the moment.'
   5 3/three singles. 'and I'm looking for a house with three bedrooms for me and my two friends.' 'OK, so that's <u>three singles</u>.'
   6 city centre. 'Do you want to live on the outskirts of town?' 'No, we'd like to live in the <u>centre</u>. We haven't got cars and we need to get to the shops and the university.'

Understanding letters and numbers p. 8

1 1 /ei/, as in p<u>ay</u>: J, K, A, H,
   2 /i:/, as in b<u>ee</u>: C, D, E, T, B, G, P, V
   3 /e/, as in <u>e</u>gg: M, N, X, F, L, S, Z
   4 /ai/, as in fl<u>y</u>: I, Y
   5 /eu/, as in n<u>o</u>: O
   6 /u:/, as in t<u>oo</u>: U, W, Q
   7 /a:/, as in c<u>ar</u>: R

2 1 1 B 2 C 3 A
   2 1 A 2 C 3 B
   3 1 C 2 A 3 B
   4 1 A 2 C 3 B
3 7 max. <u>£300 per month</u> 'OK, well our maximum is £300 per month, but that must include bills.'
   8 15 October/October 15th 'Well, we're in September now, so if you want the house for nine months, your rent will be starting in October.' 'Yes, my friends arrive in England from Spain on <u>October 15th</u>.'
   9 07788 976364 'No problem, I'll be in touch … Oh, nearly forgot. Do you have a phone number?' 'Yes, but only a mobile, it's <u>07788 976364</u>.'
   10 c.minguez@granadino.es '… And your email?' 'Um, it's <u>c.minguez@granadino.es</u>.'

Avoiding mistakes p. 8

1 Robert <u>F</u>lack ✓
2 ~~he's~~ male: too many words. Contractions count as two words.
3 twenty-one ✓
4 first y<u>ea</u>r: spelling mistake
5 John's College ✓
6 Engin<u>ee</u>ring: spelling mistake
7 BA ✓ abbreviations are acceptable if they are widely recognized.

Sentence completion: dealing with extra information p. 9

1 1 B 2 A 3 C
2 1 term 2 Basketball 3 75 / seventy-five
3 4 20/twenty. 'I was actually thinking about joining a couple – you get a <u>20% discount</u> if you join more than one.'
   5 dangerous. 'I don't know. <u>It sounds like it could be dangerous</u> and it must be difficult to make friends if you're hitting them.'
   6 lectures. 'Mmm. I'm not sure about the rowing club. I mean, I like exercise but I've heard that the rowers get up at six every day. <u>I sometimes can't get motivated</u> to get out of bed for <u>lectures that start at 9</u>!'
   7 choir. 'Yeah, me too. I think <u>choir sounds like it could be exciting</u>; I'm definitely thinking about joining that.'
   8 dancing. 'Ballroom <u>dancing</u>?! You MUST be joking!' 'Oh, come on Linda, it would be fun and anyway, it would make you light on your feet – a great skill for a basketball player to have.' <u>OK, you've convinced me</u>.'

Skills practice p. 9

1 1 B '… <u>I think there will be about 15, not including me and another tutor</u>.'
   2 B … they're second year undergraduates, so between <u>nineteen and twenty years old</u>.'
2 3 3rd September/ 3 September/ September 3rd / September 3. <u>We'll try to book plane tickets on Saturday 3rd</u> and travel back on the following Saturday.'

4 10th September/ 10 September/ September 10th / September 10 'The tenth of September?' 'That's right.'

5 7 / seven '... So we'll need accommodation for seven nights.'

6 690/six hundred and ninety 'Right, well, you could try Charles Bridge Hostel; it's right near the centre and it's quite reasonable, about 690 koruna or 30 euros per person per night.'

7 25/ twenty-five 'It's actually a bit cheaper, 25 euros a night, so that's about the same in pounds sterling.'

8 486 899 666 'Charles Bridge Hostel is on 486 899 666.'

9 castlehostel@prahaworld.ch 'It's probably better to send the Castle Hostel an email. It's castlehostel@prahaworld.ch.'

10 12 p.m. / midnight 'They're open from 9 until late. You can ring up to midnight.'

Completing a flow chart: listening for key words p. 10

1 b The key word here is 'phase' which indicates a period of time.

2 1 Honeymoon phase, period, two weeks
2 Culture shock, frustrated, foreign country
3 Coping: teach, culture
4 ingredients, local, favourite meal
5 things, like, England
6 Acceptance, knowing, life, UK

3 1 Student's own answers.   2 yes   3 no

4 1 positive. The first phase is the most positive. That's why a lot of people call it the 'honeymoon phase'.
2 angry. This is the second phase of the process, 'culture shock'. ... When this happens, a lot of foreign students feel angry or frustrated and they stay with other people from their country because it seems safer.
3 language. One student I know offered to teach an English person about her language and culture.
4 cook. Another thing you can do is to cook your favourite dishes using ingredients you buy locally, and then invite all your new friends round.
5 Find. Get out there and find all the things you do like about living here.
6 Happy. This doesn't mean that you understand everything about England but that you know what makes you happy.

Labelling a map: using visual clues p. 11

1 1 B The cathedral
2 C The town hall

2 1 Millenium Square / New Way
2 New Street Station
3 The car park
4 St Mary's Hospital

3 1 in front of reception
2 doors: to the right of reception, east side of the building
corridor: leading east from the reception doors
3 Students should tick: staff, Audiology, North, Clinical, Reception

4 At the moment, you are situated here, just in front of the reception in the main entrance. To the north of here are the staff apartments, where you'll be staying while you work here. If you go through the double doors to the right of reception and head east along the corridor, you come to the Accident and Emergency ward or A&E for short.

5 1 main entrance. 'At the moment, you are situated here, just in front of the reception in the main entrance.'
2 apartments. 'To the north of here are the staff apartments, where you'll be staying while you work here.'
3 emergency. 'If you turn right and go through the doors, you come to the Accident and Emergency ward or A&E for short.'
4 bus stops. 'To the south of the Audiology Clinic, across the road, you'll find eight bus stops.'
5 school. 'So, to continue, behind the bus stops, on the right of the map is the Clinical School.'
6 hospital. 'Between this and the Rosie Hospital at the other end of the site are the wards, where most of the patients sleep.'
7 lifts. 'Between Wards D and E is a set of lifts – these small squares here– which will take you up to the second floor and wards M–Z.'
8 car park. 'If so, you can leave your car in the staff car park, to the west of reception. I hope that's all clear. Has anyone got any questions?'

Skills practice p. 12

1 Welcome. 'Our first task is to be at Halls of Residence to welcome them and show them to their rooms.'
2 Central Hall. 'Your second task is to show small groups of students the main facilities like the library, doctors and the Central Hall.'
3 student card. 'When the tour is finished, please bring your students to the main hall. Here, they'll sign some important forms and pick up their student card.'
4 college canteens. 'After that, you need to take them to the college canteens for an evening meal.'
5 Central Hall. 'Here's a map showing the tour route we'd like you to take around the university campus. I'd like everyone to meet here at midday, at the Central Hall.'
6 bridge. 'When you leave the hall, please go through the main entrance and cross the bridge across the lake.'
7 Central Library. 'Have a quick look around the Central Library and then go north-east, towards the Science Block.'
8 Science Block. 'Have a quick look around the Central Library and then go north-east, towards the Science Block.'
9 Students' Centre. 'If you have any science students, show them the laboratories and then turn right and go south towards the Students' Centre.'
10 bus stops. 'While you're there, it's probably a good idea to show them where the bus stops are across the road so that they can catch the bus into town.'
11 Halls. 'Then, to end the tour, head behind the Central Hall towards the Halls of Residence.'
12 leisure centre. 'It's a good idea to show them the computer rooms and leisure centre to the north of there.'

Multiple choice: listening for detail and synonyms p. 13

1 1 essay   A fascinating   B topic   C marks
2 B   presentation   C modern

2 1 B 'It's this end of year essay. You said that we can write about one of the nine topics we've studied this term, but I don't know which one to choose.'
2 C 'But there are hundreds of books on modern art and lots you could write about.'

Short answers: listening for detail p. 13

1 1 D You said that we can write about one of <u>the nine topics we've studied</u> this term ...

2 B ... the seminar on <u>19th-century</u> art really made me think about what the word 'modern' means...

3 C 'Well, I didn't do very well on the <u>photography course</u>; I only got <u>60%</u> for my essay'

4 A 'But there are <u>hundreds</u> of books on modern art and lots you could write about.'

2 1 industry
2 two

Matching: identifying opinions p. 13

1 Interested in the subject: 5
Has doubts about the subject: 2, 3, 4
Not interested in the subject: 1

2 1 B   2 A   3 B

3 1 C '...impressionist painters, like Claude Monet. I'd prefer not to write about the same paintings again.'

2 B 'I'm sure you're right, but I'm having trouble thinking of ideas.'

3 A 'Well, there's lots of 21st-century artists who use unusual materials to make art... ' '... I'll definitely research that further.'

Skills practice p. 14

1 B '<u>The thing I did have problems with was my work-life balance</u>. I found that I had no time at all after preparing lessons and marking homework to relax.'

2 C 'Have you tried to get students to find things out for themselves? Perhaps you could get them to do some project work, so that they take responsibility for their own learning?'

3 C 'I can lend you a couple of books if you like.' (Josh)
'I'd suggest then, you read some books that give advice about managing time...' (Claire)

D 'Like Claire, I really like the students and I think they feel the same.' (Josh)
'Well, at first I thought that I'd have trouble with the students, but actually, they were all really easy to deal with.' (Claire)

F 'Yeah, they were great; such an intelligent group of students. I hardly had to encourage them at all.' (Claire)
'I really like the students and I think they feel the same.' (Josh)
Incorrect options: A = just Josh so far   E = just Josh
B = just Josh

4 C 'Oh, that's a shame. ... But I'm making some progress with the kids at this school.' (Josh)

5 E 'OK, well, it'll certainly be a challenge. I'm a bit worried about one of the students though ...' (Claire)

6 A 'I really think that next term will give you some valuable experience. I'm sure you'll do very well.' (tutor)

Recognizing paraphrasing p. 15

1 1 overate
2 put on
3 work out
4 disorders
5 unhealthy

2 1 problems, disorders, girls, magazines
2 women, children, gained
3 over, 70/seventy, sugary, problems
4 sitting, computer, exercise
5 overate, women, 20s/twenties

3 1 G 'You've already heard talks from my classmates on diabetes and eating problems or 'eating disorders' among teenage girls who are influenced by images in <u>magazines</u>.'

2 F 'They thought that they put on weight because of a bad diet; <u>they spent all their time looking after their children and not enough time thinking about their choice of food.</u>'

3 A 'Interestingly, these people were aware that sugary, fatty food could lead to weight problems but chose an unhealthy diet because it gave them, they thought, <u>a better quality of life</u>.'

4 B 'After <u>a long day in the office</u>, they felt too tired to work out at the gym.'

5 D 'They said that their weight went up and down, depending on whether they were going through a good or difficult <u>period of their lives</u>. '

4 A because it <u>gave them</u>, they thought, <u>a better quality of life.</u>
B <u>worked ten to twelve hours a day</u> / <u>a long day in the office</u>
D depending on whether they were going through a <u>good or difficult period</u> of their lives
E <u>didn't exercise enough</u>
F <u>they spent all their time looking after their children and not enough time thinking about their choice of food.</u>
G teenage girls <u>who are influenced by images in magazines</u>.

Completing a summary: recognizing differences in sentence structure p. 16

1 In summary completion tasks, the order of words in sentences on the question paper is usually <u>*different to*</u> the order of words in the listening.
1 C   2 D   3 A   4 B

2 1 world
2 height
3 low
4 children
5 age
6 location
7 city

Completing notes: predicting word class p. 17

1 1 C Key words: *bones, bird, dinosaurs* (and the notes are written in the past tense)

2 a bird; the text also mentions *ostrich, elephant bird, giant moa*

2 a 5   b 10   c 4   d 2

3 Gap 1 needs a noun (after a preposition).
Gap 3 needs a number (after a number but before a noun).
Gap 6 needs a noun (before a verb and a compliment).
Gap 7 needs a number (before a unit of measurement).
Gap 8 needs a comparative adjective (before *than*).
Gap 9 needs an adjective (after verb *to be*) As heading is *comparisons*, could be a comparative adjective.

4 1 desert
2 belong
3 million
4 birds
5 chicken
6 head
7 three/3
8 bigger
9 heavier
10 fly

Recognizing topic sentences p. 18

1 1 E 2 D 3 A 4 C 5 B

Skills practice p. 18

1 1 customer. 'Marketing involves thinking about what the customer wants and needs...'
2 long. 'they might think about how long the product will last. This is called its durability.'
3 fashionable. 'Or the customer might think about the style of the shoes, whether they are fashionable.'
4 key. 'Marketers need to consider who the typical consumer is for a product and whether this consumer belongs to a bigger group of people who would buy the product. This group is the product's key market.'
5 advertising. 'As you are all consumers, you'll all be aware of advertising.'
6 selling. 'But this is just one of the areas that fashion marketers work in. They also work in product development, branding, pricing, publicity, sales promotion, selling and forecasting.'

2 7 public. 'The area of fashion marketing you choose to work in will depend on your interests and skills. If you enjoy meeting members of the public, market research may be for you.'
8 managers. 'Another exciting role is marketing manager. Imagine you want to sell a shirt to a particular chain of stores.'
9 sells. 'You have to make sure that the shirt goes with other items of clothing that the store sells.'
10 boring. 'I've been working in this industry for twenty years and it's definitely not boring.'
11 hard. 'If you decide to train as a fashion marketer though, you will need to prepare yourself for hard work.'
12 experience. 'My advice to you is to get some unpaid work experience while you are training.'

Key for Reading module

Quiz p. 19

1 1 three
2 forty
3 one
4 sixty
2 False. You don't have extra time to write your answers on the answer sheet at the end of the exam.
3 True. Questions ask you to label a diagram or a map or complete a table/flow chart.

4 1 A Each reading passage in the exam is between 700 and 800 words long. The texts in this book are generally shorter than this. After you have practised the reading task with shorter texts, you can try to read longer and longer texts.
2 C Reading passages are from books, magazines, journals and newspapers. Letters are only in the General Training IELTS test.
5 A 4   B 6   C 5   D 2   E 3   F 1

Getting a general understanding of the passage p. 19

1 1 currency
2 words that relate to money: poorest, virtual money, economic, bank notes, value, $10 to $100
3 words that relate to technology: online computer game, social impact game, virtual, social networking sites

Matching headings to paragraphs p. 20

1 The passage has five paragraphs and it needs five headings. The question will have more headings than you need.

2 i A game that makes money
ii Investigation of financial benefits
iii The creation of unusual friendships
iv New game with a social purpose
v Success at an early stage of the project
vi The way the game works
vii Strategies for using social networking sites
viii Charities that benefit from the project
ix Success at a late stage of the project

3 The third piece of underlined information explains why Macon Money was invented: 'to bring people from different economic backgrounds closer together by encouraging them to meet.' If you are looking for a reason or purpose, it's a good idea to look for the words 'in order to' or 'to'.

4 Paragraph B matches heading vi, because the whole paragraph explains how the game works. The paragraph mentions social networking sites, but only to say that they are used in the game. It doesn't explain how they work.

5 C iii   D v   E ii

True, False or Not Given: understanding the difference p. 21

1 1 A virtual
2 B local
3 C college students/elderly people
4 D no, the passage doesn't specify how many old and young people play Macon Money. It just talks about these age groups in general.

2 1 TRUE. The information in the passage agrees with this statement.
2 FALSE. The information in this passage means the opposite of this statement: (local means the shops in and around the town, not across the whole country).
3 NOT GIVEN. The passage does not have information about who has won the most money.

3 1 TRUE. A 'The 92,000 people who live in Macon, Georgia, USA know each other a little better than they did, thanks to an online computer game.'
2 FALSE. B 'In the game, winning players receive "bonds", which they can then exchange for bank notes of Macon Money. ... The bonds range in value from $10 to $100.'

3 NOT GIVEN. C 'Pairs might spend their money separately, or do something together like share a meal or give the money to someone who needs it more, ...'

4 FALSE. C 'The game's designers are hoping Macon Money will bring members of the community together...'

5 FALSE. C 'says Beverly Blake of the John S. and James L. Knight Foundation, the <u>non-profit group</u> based in Miami, Florida, that funded the game.'

6 FALSE. D 'Although Macon Money is quite a new innovation, early signs are positive. The first round of the game has seen <u>$65,000-worth of bonds given out</u> and 2,688 participants so far <u>spending $48,000</u> in Macon Money.'

7 TRUE. E 'An independent research firm will now evaluate how much economic activity the game has caused, with results due later this year.'

Yes, No or *Not Given* questions: recognizing the claims of the writer p. 22

1 A opinion: written in the first person eg 'I feel very positive ...'
   B claim: backed up by Darwin's scientific theories
   C opinion: adverb such as 'unfortunately' shows what writer feels
   D claim: supported by research: 'According to researchers...' 'Dr Donald Broom, a professor at Cambridge University, says ...'

2 3 Similarities between elephants and humans revealed.

3 *argues that*: 'the study argues that we definitely share similar emotional reactions and thought processes with elephants.'
   claims that: 'that claims that human beings have certain characteristics in common with elephants.'
   conclude that: 'Her findings, published by University of Chicago Press conclude that there is "no doubt" that elephants display empathy for one another.'
   demonstrates: 'For instance, the study demonstrates that elephants feel upset when another elephant is in pain, feel angry over disagreements and can recognize members of their family.'
   describes: 'The study describes elephants touching trunks or bumping shoulders in greeting, while "playful" elephants moved their heads from side to side to start a game.'
   details evidence of: 'The project also details evidence of elephants' higher thinking skills.'
   reveals : 'However, the study – the Amboseli elephant research project – reveals for the first time the range of emotions that elephants can show.'
   proved that: 'Scientists have even proved that their short-term memories are better than humans' in some respects.'
   found to be: 'They have been found to be more intelligent than apes in some areas, such as route planning.'

4 1 a appearance
      b think (thought processes)
      c yes: 'we share similar emotional reactions and thought processes with elephants'
   2 a angry, upset, sadness
      b observe
      c the different types of elephant emotions: 'reveals for the first time the range of emotions that elephants can show'
   3 a emotions
      b their bodies/body language
      c no
      Answers are: 1 YES   2 NO   3 NOT GIVEN

5 1 NO. The body language that elephants use is familiar to humans, not the other way round.
      'The body language used by elephants is also recognizable to humans'.

   2 YES. 'In addition, the researchers thought they saw evidence of "conversation" between the elephants; when the signal to move was given, elephants stood side by side and "discussed" which route to take. When this long exchange ended, the elephants moved all together in one direction.'

   3 NOT GIVEN. The passage says that they have a good memory but doesn't say anything about their sense of direction: 'Elephants also have ... the knowledge to remember routes through the landscape many years after they last travelled them. They have been found to be more intelligent than apes in some areas, such as route planning.'

   4 YES. 'They have been found to be more intelligent than apes in some areas, such as route planning, while other experiments have shown them as capable as monkeys in co-operating on tasks. Scientists have even proved that their short-term memories are better than humans' in some respects.'

   5 NO. 'There is considerable support for her findings.'

Skills practice p. 24

1 A ix Paragraph A includes several dates from different times in history.
2 B iv 'That's what historians have always believed. However ...'
3 C iii '... when the object was found, it was stored in a box marked "wooden bird model" ... As a result of their findings, the object was displayed in the museum of Cairo as a "model aeroplane".'
4 D ii '... this object seems to suggest otherwise, despite the refusal of unimaginative science to accept the evidence.'
5 E v 'Gold trinkets discovered in Central America and coastal areas of South America are further evidence of early flight.'
6 F vi 'flying vehicles are written about in early texts... There is no shortage of descriptions of flying machines in ancient sources.'
7 FALSE. 'It wasn't until the Wright brothers made their first successful flights of *Kitty Hawk* in 1903 that powered flight became a reality.'
8 FALSE. 'However, a small minority of researchers and scientists have re-examined historical objects and have found evidence to suggest that humans achieved flight earlier than 20th century.'
9 FALSE. 'A strange flying object was found in 1898 in a tomb at Saqquara, Egypt and was later dated around 200 BCE ... The object was later re-discovered by Dr Khalil Messiha...'
10 NOT GIVEN. Concorde is referred to but there is no mention of scientists comparing it to the Egyptian model aeroplane; the comparison is made by the author: 'The curved shape and size of the glider's wings are behind its ability to fly; a similar type of curving wings can be seen on Concorde and gave the plane maximum "lift" without a reduction in speed.'
11 FALSE. 'But this object seems to suggest otherwise, despite the refusal of unimaginative science to accept the evidence.'
12 TRUE. 'The archaeologists who discovered them labelled these objects as *zoomorphic*, meaning animal shaped, but it is unclear which animal they represent.'
13 NOT GIVEN. Arthur Young was a 'designer of Bell helicopters and other aircraft'; he may have built a plane but the text does not say so.
14 TRUE. '... flying vehicles are written about in early texts ...'

Using information in a table p. 25

1 a The word 'analysis' is the heading of the first column of the table.

b The word 'analysis' occurs in each paragraph of the passage.

c Words next to analysis: infrared, canvas, brush-stroke, computer

d Types of analysis should all go in the first column of the table in the same order that they occur in the passage.

2 a First word in bold in column 2 of the table is 'famous', in 'Expert' analysis row of the table. This type of analysis is described in paragraph B of the passage. A synonym of 'famous' is 'well-known', in paragraph B.

b The word 'well-known' appears in the following sentence: 'who used their experience to analyze the look of a painting and decide whether it matched the style of a **well-known** artist.'

c The gap in the sentence in the table needs a noun: the sentence already has a subject and a verb (matches) so it needs an object. The word 'style' is already in the sentence in the table, so this can't be the answer. 'the look' of the painting is matched to the 'style' of the artist in the passage, so the answer must be 'look'.

d Limited: Experts can't **date** (2) .... or see through paint.
Refers to 'Expert analysis': paragraph B
Synonym of 'date' (verb) in passage: 'identify the age'
Word needed in gap: noun (follows verb)
words around synonym in passage: 'The human eye cannot identify the age of the materials used, or see underneath the paint to the canvas that the artist painted on.'
answer: materials

Looked at (3) .... **below** Italian painting
Refers to 'Infrared analysis': paragraph C
Synonym of 'below' (preposition) in passage: 'underneath'
Word needed in gap: noun (following a preposition – at – needs an object)
words around synonym in passage: 'By analyzing the painting with infrared, scientists discovered that the drawing **underneath** the painting was done in pencil, a material which wasn't available in the 15th century'.
answer: drawing

Quantity and (9) .... of strokes counted by a program.
Refers to 'Brush stroke analysis': paragraph E
Synonym of 'quantity' (noun) in passage: 'number'
Word needed in gap: noun, probably abstract (same class of word as 'quantity')
words around synonym in passage: 'A computer program studies the colours used by a particular artist and counts the number and combination of brush strokes used across a paintings.'
answer: combination

3 a The first word in italics is 'discovery'. It relates to 'Expert analysis', dealt with in paragraph B of the table.

b different forms of 'discovery' could be 'discover', 'discovered' (verbs)

c 'Of course, it's possible for forgers to avoid being discovered by infrared analysis...'

d Word needed in gap: verb (follows the subject of the sentence 'forgers'). Verb in sentence in passage, before 'being discovered': 'avoid'

4 1 look
2 materials
3 Infrared
4 drawing
5 avoid
6 X-ray
7 number / quantity
8 accurate
9 Brush stroke
10 combination

Using information in a diagram p. 27

1 There are four labels that you have to complete. Four parts of the eye are already labelled.

2 1 the verb 'to see' relates to 'vision'.
2 receiving light and sending electrical messages: 'some parts receive light into the eye and some send electrical impulses, or messages, which communicate an image of what we are looking at to our brains.'

3 a The pupil is in the middle of the iris. 'The pupil ... is in the middle of a coloured circle, called the iris.'
b The retina is at the back of the eye. '... controlling the direction of the light so that it is reaches the right place at the back of the eye. This area is called the retina.'
c Muscles go behind the eye. 'Six muscles attached to the sides of the eye and going behind it allow it to move at an angle of 180 degrees but prevent the eye rolling backwards.'
d The sclera is on the outside of the eye. 'The white layer around the outside of the eye, called the sclera, protects the delicate insides of the eye from danger by preventing small objects from getting into the eye.'

4 A iris. 'The iris makes the pupil reduce in size ... The amount of light that goes into the eye is controlled by the changing size of the pupil ...'
B sclera. 'The white layer around the outside of the eye, called the sclera, protects the delicate insides of the eye from danger by preventing small objects from getting into the eye.'
C pupil. 'The pupil is a black hole which allows light into the eye.'
D muscles. 'Six muscles attached to the sides of the eye and going behind it allow it to move at an angle of 180 degrees but prevent the eye rolling backwards.'
E retina. 'The retina converts light into electrical messages.'

5 1 & 2 Students' answers will vary.

6

Sentence completion: recognizing word class and synonyms p. 28

1 1 a, noun (could be plural or abstract, not requiring an article)
  2 b, verb, present
  3 a, plural noun (to match rods)
  4 a, plural noun (to correspond with verb 'stop')
  5 a, plural noun (to follow adjectives 'tiny, airborne')

2 1 daylight. 'They recognize colour and detail and need daylight to **work well**.'
  2 transmit. 'Rods ... do not recognize colours. They transmit information in **black and white** to the brain.'
  3 cones. 'Rods **outnumber** cones; there are approximately 120 million of them in the eye. It is the rods which help us to "see in the dark".'
  4 Muscles. 'Six muscles ... allow it to move at an angle of 180 degrees but **prevent** the eye rolling backwards.'
  5 objects. 'Because the eye is open to the outside world, **small** objects can **fly** into it. Eyelashes stop this from happening.'

3 Both answers are incorrect because they don't use the words in the passage. Sentence 2 should use the word 'transmit' rather than 'send' and sentence 5 should use the word 'objects' rather than 'things'. Sentence 5 also uses two words where one is required, and 'small' is a repetition of 'tiny'.

Summary completion: passive sentences p. 29

1 1 No, the subject of the summary sentence is 'The changing size of the pupil'; the subject of sentence A is 'The amount of light that goes into the eye'.
  2 The summary uses present simple, sentence A uses *be* + past participle.
  3 The summary sentence is an active sentence; sentence A is a passive sentence.

2 C 'which are then sent to the brain along the optic nerve.'
Summary: 'Black and white information is transmitted to the brain by ...'
'The eye is protected both by our eyelashes and ...'

3 Gap 2: verb in *-ing* form as it follows a preposition
Gap 3: noun, following definite article *the*
Gap 4: noun, object, following the verb *transmitted*. As sentence is in the passive, the object will be the 'doer' of the action i.e. what transmits the information to the brain?
Gap 5: adjective, before another adjective (*protective*) and before a noun (*layer*)

4 2 contracting
  3 optic nerve
  4 rods
  5 white

Skills practice p. 30

1 1 pod(s)
  2 The Olmecs
  3 savoury
  4 currency
  5 sweet
  6 wedding
  7 chocolate houses

2 1 apricots
  2 accident
  3 (small) rabbit
  4 (wedding) guests
  5 expensive

3 6 D 7 G 8 A 9 H 10 C

Multiple choice questions: reading the question p. 32

1 Paragraphs A, B and E. The writer's thoughts and opinions are important in questions 2 and 3.

2 i The second question 'Why is there damage to the environment?'
  ii No, the text says Rizhao is 'preparing to get much bigger': this is talking about the future. The paragraph says more about China's development than Rizhao's.
  iii Roads are referred to in paragraph A: 'The road into town is eight lanes wide, even though at the moment there's not much traffic.' There isn't a clear link between roads specifically and greenhouse gases in the paragraph.
  iv Iron is referred to in paragraph A: '... large quantities of iron arrive every day by ship.' The effect that iron has on the environment isn't specified.
  v Yes: 'The growth of cities increases the amount of harmful greenhouse gas released into the atmosphere. It's this kind of expansion that has increased the production of global warming gases in China.' The writer describes greenhouse gases as 'harmful' which is a synonym for 'damaging'. Option D is therefore the correct answer.

3 i 'a reason' has a similar meaning to 'purpose'.
  ii Paragraph B doesn't give examples of problems so option A probably isn't correct.
  iii 'Environmentally friendly' has a positive meaning. Solar energy is mentioned. The paragraph talks about the 'whole of China', as well as Rizhao: 'And it's not just Rizhao which is spending money on renewable, environmentally friendly energy, the whole of China is number 1 in the world for using renewable energy technology.' Option B, therefore, is probably not correct.
  iv There is only one phrase connected with the economy in paragraph B: 'spending money'. This phrase doesn't talk about the economy in itself but specifies that the money is being invested in being environmentally friendly. Option C therefore is not correct.
  v 'The whole of China is number 1 in the world for using renewable energy technology.' This emphasizes China's achievements in protecting the environment. This is the correct option.

4 i 'the future'. The date in the paragraph is 2030.
  ii 'excited' is similar to 'optimistic'. The writer doesn't seem excited about the future. He describes the picture of the future as 'dark'. Option A isn't correct.
  iii The writer does offer solutions to the environmental problems, eg international collaboration. So the situation isn't hopeless. Option B therefore isn't correct.
  iv The sentence 'It's a dark picture' indicates that the writer is concerned, or 'pessimistic' about the scientists' predictions. This option is therefore correct.
  v The final line of paragraph E suggests that the writer feels personally involved in the problem of global warming: 'In the end, no one country can take full responsibility for saving the environment; we are all responsible.' Option D therefore is not correct.

Recognizing synonyms p. 33

1 There are three correct answers.

2 Number of people ... increasing = growing population; fossil fuels = oil, coal and gas; new jobs = fresh employment opportunities; more money = greater wealth; energy-hungry = demand for power; rapidly = quickly

3 energy = power; needs to grow = need to develop; spending their money = buy

4 B not correct. The paragraph mentions fossil fuels but doesn't say that there is a shortage.

   C correct. China's economy needs to grow by 8% a year and the government needs to produce fresh job opportunities for the growing population.

   D correct. People with 'greater wealth' are 'spending their money on technology', the 'demand for power is increasing'.

   E correct. Refers to the 'growing populations of the new cities'.

Matching features: recognizing paraphrasing p. 35

1 In matching tasks, the categories are in the same order as the order they appear in the passage.

2 1 'One fifth' is similar to '20 percent'; 'without work' is another way of saying 'unemployed'. Sentence A refers to 'the unemployment rate'.

   2 The same words are used in both sentences but the sentences are constructed differently.

   3 'improved' is similar to 'recover'; 'the economic situation' is similar to 'the economy'.

3 Sentence 1 uses technique ii.
     Sentence 2 uses technique i.
     Sentence 3 uses technique iii.

4 1 C   2 D   3 E   4 B   5 C   6 A   7 B

Skills practice p. 37

1 1 C   2 D   3 B

2 A, B, C, F, G

3 A 4, 7   B 2, 6   C 5   D 1, 3

Key for Writing module

Quiz p. 38

1 1 The writing module lasts for **60** minutes.

   2 You should spend **20** minutes on Task 1.

   3 You should spend **40** minutes on Task 2.

   4 You should write at least **150** words for Task 1.

   5 You should write at least **250** words for Task 2.

2 Task 1: D a description of a process,
     F a description of data in a graph, chart or table
     Task 2: A an essay giving opinions or responding to a problem

3 B, D, E, G
     You don't get more marks if you:

   A have neat handwriting. However, if the examiner cannot read your writing, you will lose marks.

   C write a lot more than the number of words suggested. The examiner will stop marking your writing after they have read up to the recommended number of words.

   F include as much detail as possible in your answers. The detail you include needs to be relevant and help you to explain the main point.

Understanding graphs: choosing the most important information p. 38

1 a FALSE. The numbers on the vertical axis represent money in pounds sterling.

   b TRUE

   c TRUE

   d TRUE

   e FALSE. People in Wales earned about 50 pounds more in 2010 than in 2007.

   f TRUE

   g FALSE. In the year 2001, in England the average amount earned per week was about 60 pounds more than the amount earned in Wales in the same year.

2 Important, general information: statements c, d and f. More detailed information: statements e and g

Describing data p. 39

1 1 D   2 B   3 D   4 E   5 D   6 E   7 E   8 D
     9 E   10 E   11 A   12 E   13 B   14 C   15 E   16 E

2 A lowest
     B much
     C higher
     D overall
     E just, a little, quite

3 1 The example answer includes *some* of the numbers in the graph.

   2 Numbers are included *after* a statement is made about the graph.

   3 Numbers support *important* points, for example the biggest, or smallest piece of information.

Structuring a chart description p. 40

1 1 C   2 A   3 D   4 B

2 A ranging between six and nine percent
     C Together, these constitute 73 percent
     D at just over 40 percent; at just over 30%.

3 1 B   2 D   3 A   4 C

Writing an introduction to a graph description p. 41

1 amount of money earned = wages; jobs = occupations; every year = annual

2 1 C   2 D   3 A   4 B

3 1 graduated = completed their studies; discipline = subject; higher education = university

   2 participated = took part

   3 global = around the world; literacy rate = percentage of men and women who could read and write

   4 typical = average; quarterly = every three months

Skills practice p. 42

Model answer

The bar graph shows the number of people who used the Internet in different areas of the world in 2011. By far the greatest number of Internet users were in Asia, at 922.3 million. Just over half of this number of people used the Internet in Europe, at 476.2 million. Oceania / Australia had the lowest number of Internet users at just over 20 million.

Describing changes over time p. 42

1 A Figure 3 B Figure 1 C Figure 2

2 and **3**

	(Adjective +) noun	Verb (+ adverb/ adjective)
↗	a rise / an increase	to rise
↘	a fall / a decline	to fall
↑	a sharp rise (*a dramatic rise* also possible)	to rise dramatically
↘	a steady decline (*a steady fall* also possible)	to decline steadily
→	n.a.	*to remain stable*
→	a slight increase	to increase slightly
↗	a steady rise (*a gradual increase* also possible)	to rise steadily
∿↗	a fluctuation	to fluctuate

3 Note the tense use: past simple to describe a change over time which finished in the past:
Between 1990 and 1995 the percentage **fell** by 3% and the same fall **occurred** between 1995 and 2000.
Use the present perfect to describe a change over time which continues until now:
The number of people in the world who do not have clean water to drink **has declined steadily** since 1990.

Comparing data to show change p. 44

1 1 D   2 B   3 C   4 A
2 Sentence A is supported by information in sentence 2. Sentence C is supported by information in sentences 1, 3 and 4.

Comparing two sets of data p. 45

1 **The best opening statement** is C because it mentions both sets of data in the graphs (UK and London) and paraphrases the title of the graph.

2 The best answer is B. To describe every piece of information in each graph will take too much time. You need to choose the most important information to compare in both graphs.

3 *however, in contrast, whereas. However* and *in contrast* often go at the beginning of a sentence.

Skills practice p. 46
Model answer
These two sets of data compare the time taken for commuters in the UK and in London to travel to work with the average amount of money earned by the same commuters per hour.

A large proportion of London commuters (40 per cent) travel for between half an hour and an hour to get to work, compared to just 17 per cent of commuters in the rest of the UK. In contrast, 46 per cent of workers outside London travel for less than 15 minutes whereas only 18 percent of London commuters have such a short journey time.

The second graph shows that there is also a difference between the amount of money earned by London employees and those working in the rest of the UK, with those working in London earning between approximately £2 and £5 more.

Overall, the graph shows that the longer the journey time, the more an employee earns; employees in London who travelled for more than an hour earned around £18 whereas those who travelled for a quarter of an hour earned approximately half of this sum. The same applies to commuters living in the rest of the UK.

Organizing your writing p. 46

1 The description starts at the 'Evaporation' point of the diagram – when water evaporates from the sea. This is a good place to start as the reader will understand where the water comes from originally.

2 1 TRUE.
  2 FALSE. You should separate stages of the diagram into different paragraphs
  3 TRUE. As this is a diagram of a cycle, there isn't really a general pattern to describe.

3 A When, as
  B After that
  C Once
  D Eventually

Choosing between the active and passive p. 47

1 A *When* water is heated by the sun, it evaporates from the ocean into the atmosphere. It also rises into the atmosphere from plants and trees.
  B *Eventually*, the water in the clouds falls back down to earth.
  C The water is used by trees and plants.
  1 is heated; is used
  2 The water is the subject of all the sentences.
  3 The water is the most important thing in each of the sentences and in the description.

2 1 b   2 b   3 b

Describing a map p. 48

1 1 Type 1: a map that shows two or more possible locations for something
  2 A new airport
  3 The town of Stanford
  4 In the nature reserve

2 Yes.

3 ... This may disturb residents of the town, ~~which is a shame.~~
... some trees would need to be cut down, ~~causing terrible environmental damage,~~ ...
... For safety reasons, the site in the nature reserve would probably be better for the people of Stanford. ~~And after all, people are more important than animals.~~

Skills practice p. 49

Model answer

This diagram illustrates the process of making and packaging liquorice. Liquorice is a sweet made from wheat flour, black juice, aniseed oil, sugar and salt. Other ingredients are also used. First of all, the ingredients to make liquorice are put into a high pressure cooker. They are then mixed together and cooked in order to make them into a paste. The heated paste is taken out of the cooker and before it has cooled, it is pushed through an extruder so that it's made into a long, thin piece of liquorice. This long piece of liquorice is then put onto a conveyor belt to cool. Once the liquorice strand has cooled, it passes along the conveyor belt and is cut up into pieces by a cutter. After that, the liquorice pieces are painted with a liquid, called a glaze. Finally, the liquorice pieces are packaged in plastic in order to be sold to consumers.

Skills development: analyzing the question and identifying the essay type p. 50

1 A 9   B 5   C 4   D 1, 2

2 Example notes
B In some countries – *which?*
alternative routes to employment – *some alternatives: apprenticeships, start at the bottom of a company and work up*
To what extent do you think this is a positive or negative development? – *how far do I agree or disagree that this is positive?*
C 'age that people can retire is increasing' – *finish work later*
'advantages' – *keep active, more experience, stay independent.*
'disadvantages' – *tired/stressed, difficult to learn new skills, expensive for employers*
D 'behavioural problems' – *e.g. becoming withdrawn, believing reality and virtual world the same.*
'solutions' – *limit to computer time? censor unsuitable material? discussions in lessons at school?*

3 1 A   2 C   3 D   4 B

Planning an essay p. 51

1 1 Plan A only discusses the disadvantages of later retirement.
2 In Plan C, the conclusion repeats the introduction.
3 In Plan A, the essay gives information that the essay question doesn't require: the conclusion offers solutions.

2 Plan B is the most appropriate.

Structuring the essay p. 52

1 1 D Main points: 'age of retirement in a number of countries around the world has been increased by the government. This is partly because people are living longer and so need to work for longer to have enough money when they retire. This has caused unrest in some countries.'

Examples: 'For example, in France and England there have been strikes.'
Link to next paragraph: 'There are further disadvantages to an increased retirement age, as well as a number of advantages.'
2 C Main point: 'One disadvantage is that people will have less time to enjoy life. Consequently, workers could suffer from health issues such as stress. A further disadvantage of an older workforce is that they may find it difficult to learn new skills, ...'
Example: 'such as how to use new technology.'
Main point: 'Also, the more senior workers there are in a company, the fewer jobs there will be for young people. Older workers, in addition, cost companies more because they earn more.'
Link to next paragraph: 'However, there are advantages to having more experienced workers in a company.'
3 A All key points.
4 B All key points.

2 1 An additional advantage; in addition; Also; A further disadvantage; as well as
2 Consequently; therefore
3 However; Although
4 For example; such as

3 1 Consequently / therefore
2 A further disadvantage
3 also
4 However
5 For example
6 as well as
7 such as

Skills practice p. 52

1 Example plan:
Introduction: costs more to go to university
– school leavers try to find another way to get a job
– positive and negative aspects
Positive things:
– Good for more practical people – train to learn how to become a plumber / mechanic
– Earn money straight away: independence
– Avoids huge student loans and debt
Negative aspects:
– Not suitable for those who want a more 'academic' job
– Can't compete with graduates
– short-sighted: doctors / scientists / teachers of the future?
Conclusion:
– Negative aspects outweigh positive

2 Model answer

One advantage of not going to university is that young people can start earning money immediately. This helps them to become financially independent quickly and to start saving for important things, like a house. This is impossible for graduates because many of them have to take out a loan to pay their way through university. A further advantage of going straight into work is that it provides practical people with good on-the-job training. This approach is perfect for those who need to learn skilled manual work such as plumbing. However, for other people, there are many disadvantages to missing out on university.

A disadvantage for some students is that it limits their job prospects. Without a degree, it's very difficult to enter into an academic field such as research or medicine, particularly if there's competition from graduates. This has consequences for the future; with fewer graduates, there's likely to be fewer doctors, scientists and teachers in the future.

Writing a good introduction p. 53

1   Introduction B follows the guidelines. Introduction A repeats the exam question, and introduces arguments that belong in the body of the essay (e.g. possible causes and effects).

Using a range of language p. 53

1   effects = consequences, causes = reasons
2 1 convenient
2 explanations
3 quiet
4 comfortable

Being accurate p. 54

1 1 *fewer people use buses and trains*
2 transport
3 to make a profit
4 reducing
5 worse
6 has
7 Cars
8 which

Writing an effective conclusion p. 54

1   Conclusion 1 follows the guidelines. Conclusion 2 doesn't sum up the effects of using the car and it introduces a new idea, not discussed in the main body of the essay.

Skills practice p. 54

1   **Model answer**

Introduction:

In countries such as the UK and the USA, it's becoming increasingly expensive for school leavers to study at university. This has led many young people to decide not to attend university and to find a job in a different way. In my opinion this situation has a few advantages but it also has a number of drawbacks.

Conclusion:

In conclusion, on balance I think that the disadvantages of not attending university outweigh the advantages. Although students can avoid getting into debt, they may have a disappointing career because they do not have good qualifications, and in society as a whole the result might be a shortage of qualified people in highly-skilled academic fields.

Key for Speaking module

Quiz p. 55

1   B
2   A
3 1 Part 3
2 Part 1
3 Part 2
4 Part 2
5 Part 2
6 Part 3
4   Higher score: 2, 4 and 5
Lower score: 1, 3, 6, 7 and 8

Getting started p. 55

1 1 The best answer is B because she gives her first name and surname. The other answers don't give the candidate's full name.
2 The best answer is B: it uses correct grammatical structures and gives more detail. Answer A has some grammatical mistakes and answer C is too short. One or two word answers will lose marks.
3 The best answer is A: it shows that the candidate has good conversational English. C is grammatically correct but if the candidate does not bring identification with them, they can't do the speaking exam.

Learning key vocabulary p. 56

1   **Home Town:** busy, facilities, historic, modern, population, suburbs/outskirts,
Education: degree, graduation/graduate from, qualification/qualify for, secondary school, study, subjects
Food: delicious, eat out, main course, fast food, healthy food, typical dishes
2   Student's own answers

Answering the question p. 56

1   Favourite places 1; Work 2 and 5; Leisure 3 and 6; Friends 4; Clothes 7; Food / Your country 8; Home town 9; Holidays 10; Education 11
1 When
2 What
3 What
4 How
5 Why
6 When, what
7 Is
8 How
9 Which/what
10 When
11 What

2 A: 2, 5, 7, 10 and 11
   B: 1, 3, 4, 6, 8, 9
   C: 2. The question asks about your job now not your job in the future.
   D: 4, 6

Using the correct tense p. 57

1 1 <u>Has</u> your country <u>changed</u> much since you were a child?
   C   Yes. <u>It's grown</u> from a small town to a much bigger place. All options answer the question but Option C uses the same verb form.
   2 <u>Was</u> it easy for you to get this qualification?
   B   Actually, it <u>was</u> quite difficult. I <u>had</u> to work full time and study at night.
   Answer B is best as it uses the same verb form. Answers A and C are grammatically correct but don't directly answer the question.
   3 What <u>would you like</u> to do in the future?
   C   <u>I'd like</u> to study to become a teacher and perhaps have children one day.
   Answer C is best as it uses the same verb form. Answers A and B are grammatically correct but don't answer the question.

2 Candidate: I <u>live</u> (present simple) on the outskirts of a small, historic town in south-east Germany. Um, <u>I've lived</u> (present perfect) there for twenty-three years. The town <u>has changed</u> (present perfect) quite a lot in this time. It <u>used to be</u> (*used to*) much smaller but a few years ago, a car manufacturer <u>opened</u> (past simple) on the outskirts and this <u>encouraged</u> (past simple) a lot of people to move to the town to look for jobs.

3 Candidate: Her name is Frida. *I've known* her since we *were* both at school. The funny thing is that at first we *didn't* like each other, but one day I *shouted* at a girl who was horrible to Frida and we *became* friends. We *see* each other about once a month and we always *have* a great time. *I'm going to see / I'm seeing* her next week for a very special occasion – she's getting married.

Speaking fluently p. 57

1 A What's your favourite hobby?
2 usually, sometimes, at other times, now
3 A 3   B 1   C 2
   1 but
   2 anyway
   3 because
4 1 usually
   2 because
   3 but
   4 because
   5 anyway
   6 sometimes

Skills practice p. 58

1 Candidate B gives a better answer. Candidate A hesitates more than B. Answer A also has vocabulary and grammatical mistakes (*It's an <u>interested</u> job; we <u>are getting</u> very tired at the end of term*). Their pronunciation is very difficult to understand because of their accent. They don't use connecting words.

2 Possible questions for some every day topics:
   Family: Do you have a big or a small family? Is family important to you? Why/why not? Which is more important, family or friends?
   Clothes: Do you ever buy clothes online? Do you spend more money on clothes or on other things? Do you follow fashion?
   Your country: Tell me a bit about your country. What would you suggest a tourist visits in your country?

3 Model answers:
   Is family important to you? Why/why not?
   Yes, definitely. I'm very close to my family and they have supported me when things in my life were difficult. My family also helps me to remember who I am. We share important memories together and we all come from the same place and have similar beliefs.
   Do you ever buy clothes online?
   Yes, sometimes. Internet shopping is very useful when I don't have time to go shopping or if a particular shop is online but not in my town. I think I probably shop online about once a month.
   What would you suggest a tourist visits in your country?
   There are so many things to see! First of all, I suggest that they go to the capital city, Rome. They can see the Roman ruins there and perhaps visit the Vatican City. They should also go to the coast while they are there; the Amalfi coastline is very beautiful and very famous. Of course, they shouldn't go home without visiting lots of good Italian restaurants!

Planning your answer: writing notes p. 59

1 The notes in B would be more useful. Notes in A are written in full sentences. There won't be time to do this in the exam. Also, it's tempting to read full sentences out loud, which isn't a good idea.

Introducing ideas and opinions p. 59

1 1 a   2 b   3 b
2 Students' own answers
3 **Model answer**
A restaurant I've really enjoyed eating at is 'Effi's'. The restaurant is in Istanbul, which is the place I visited last year, on holiday with my friends. We decided to go out for a meal because it was my birthday and we wanted to celebrate it. The reason why we chose Effi's was because the hotel staff recommended it to us. They said that the food was good, but not too expensive and a lot fo the locals ate there. We didn't want to eat in a restaurant full of tourists. We ate lots of different foods that night, but I remember delicious kebabs, meze and pilav, particularly. One of the things I liked about the restaurant was the atmosphere. It was very friendly and the staff wanted you to have a good time. Another thing was the food – it was the best meal out I've ever had.

Organizing your answer p. 60

1 1 C   2 B   3 A   4 D
2 A One
   B place
   C artist
   D reason
3 B

4 **Extra detail:** It's made from Italian marble, taken from the mountains near Carrara, in Tuscany. It's a very big sculpture; about five metres tall.
I learnt later that this is only a copy of the original statue. The original is in the 'Academia' gallery in Florence.
He lived and worked in the 15th century. He's a very famous artist. He made lots of amazing sculptures and he painted the Sistine Chapel in Rome, too.

5 **Model answer**
One of my favourite art works is called 'Composition VIII'. It's a painting and it was created by a Russian artist called Wassily Kandinsky. It was painted in 1923. It's difficult to describe the painting because it's abstract. It's full of shapes, such as circles, semi-circles and triangles. The shapes don't look like a photograph, they aren't three-dimensional. It all looks very flat and very colourful. The place where I first saw 'Composition VIII' was in the Guggenheim Gallery in New York when I was a music student. The reason I like the painting is that Kandinsky was trying to do something different to other artists. He was trying to paint abstract ideas on canvas, not just to copy objects from real life. Kandinsky tried to represent the sounds of music in a painting. I find that really interesting.

Using stress and intonation p. 61

1 Example B sounds more interesting because the speaker uses a variety of intonation and stresses particular words.

2 The <u>person</u> I admire <u>the most</u> is my <u>mother</u>. The <u>reason</u> I think she's <u>wonderful</u> is because she has <u>always</u> put her <u>children first</u>.

Skills practice p. 61

Model answer
Well, a place in my country which I find fascinating is Stonehenge. Um, it's a circle of huge stones which have been standing for centuries in the south-west of England. Nowadays, you can still see the stones but you can only walk near them on particular days, for example, a day called the 'summer solstice'. The reason why I find Stonehenge interesting is because it's mysterious. Nobody really knows how or why it was built all those years ago. Lots of people have different beliefs though ...

Discussing topics p. 62

1 1 A, B, F 2 D 3 C, E

2 Candidate A answers question A.
Candidate B answers question F.
Candidate C answers question C.

3 1 B 2 A 3 D 4 C

4 A 4 B 5 C 1 D 2 E 3

5 A positive
B positive
C negative
D neutral

Skills practice p. 62

Model answers
B What are the advantages and disadvantages of learning a foreign language?
Well, I think the advantages actually outweigh the disadvantages, particularly nowadays. In many countries, it's necessary to know how to communicate in a foreign language in order to do business and of course, a foreign language is really useful if you want to travel on business and on holiday.
Um, I suppose one disadvantage might be that you don't feel yourself, I mean, if you speak a language which isn't yours a lot, you sometimes lose a bit of who you are.

D What kinds of things do you think students should learn in history lessons?
This is a difficult question to answer because it depends very much on your country. Um, when I was at school, we learnt a lot about history which happened in the last century, for example, the World Wars. I found it interesting but I think history should actually tell you about your country, so you get a good idea of where you live and why you should be proud of your country. Also, I'd like to learn about history which goes back further, you know, who was the first king or queen of my country. I sometimes feel embarrassed because I don't know anything like this.

Key for Practice test

Listening

1 nine / 9
2 one / 1
3 job / work
4 £500 / five hundred pounds
5 11.30 half past eleven
6 Al-Shariff
7 October 1994
8 205 Diesel
9 YL34 GGB
10 £1,250 / one thousand, two hundred and fifty pounds
11 C
12 B
13 assignment / reading list or reading list / assignment
14 (the) Internet / internet
15 email
16 student forum
17 grade

Questions 18–20: C, E and F
21 prepared
22 listening
23 questions
24 evidence
25 concerned
26 data
27 C
28 F
29 D
30 B
31 weight
32 mass
33 146 / one hundred and forty six
34 2.3 million / 2,300,000
35 80 years / eighty years

36 straight
37 stone
38 buildings
39 60 / sixty
40 internal

Reading

1 B viii
2 C iv
3 D ii
4 E vii
5 dish / reflector
6 antenna
7 (radio) receiver
8 computer
9 TRUE
10 TRUE
11 NOT GIVEN
12 FALSE
13 FALSE
14 C
15 C
16 B
17 C
18 NO
19 YES
20 YES
21 NOT GIVEN
22 C
23 D
24 A
25 H
26 I
27 F
28 B
29 E
30 A
31 C
Questions 32–35: B, C, E, F
36 eggs
37 leaves
38 heads
39 cocoons
40 yarn

Writing

Model Answer for Task 1

The two graphs detail how many million tourists arrived in particular countries around the world. The first chart shows tourist arrivals by month, over a period of one year. In 2010, numbers of tourists started at just under 60 million and rose steadily until they reached a peak of just over 110 million in July. After that numbers fell sharply until they reached around 68 million in November. The second graph shows that in 2010 the total number of tourist arrivals reached its peak at 940 million. Overall, the greatest number of tourists flew into Europe, increasing to just under 500 million in 2010. The number of tourists visiting Asia shows a dramatic growth, from around 20 million in 1980 to 200 million in 2010, whereas the increase in tourists visiting the Americas was steadier, increasing from around 50 million in 1980 to approximately 100 million in 2010. The number of tourists in the Middle East and Africa has also grown over the period peaking at around 30 million in 2010. Overall, despite slight fluctuations in numbers, the number of tourists travelling around the world is increasing.

Model Answer for Task 2

Aeroplanes cause up to 5 per cent of the global amount of carbon dioxide, which damages the ozone layer. This has led the government to try to decrease the amount of air travel by increasing its cost. I think there are both disadvantages and advantages to the government's plans.

I will begin with the disadvantages. Because of the popularity of flying, airports are getting bigger. My local airport, for example, has doubled in size over five years. The expansion of airports creates jobs. If the number of passengers decreases, jobs may be lost. Another disadvantage is the negative impact that decreased travel will have on business. Business nowadays is global and people fly in order to make deals. If this isn't possible because flying gets too expensive, it may have a negative impact on the economy, although with the Internet, it's sometimes possible to do business online.

There is one major advantage to fewer people flying; it will help to save the environment. If we can reduce the amount of carbon dioxide released into the atmosphere, global warming will slow down. There are also more local advantages. Fewer planes means less noise pollution. There will also be less danger of our natural environment being damaged by the building of new roads and runways. If fewer people fly, it also may mean that the national tourist trade benefits.

Overall, I think that the advantages of raising the cost of air travel outweigh the disadvantages. We need to find a way of saving the environment and reducing air travel would do this both globally and locally. It may also benefit our national economy. Although sectors of business may suffer, business can be done over the Internet.

Listening module

Recording 01

[A= Accommodation officer, C = Carlos]
A: Good morning, can I help you?
C: Yes, I hope so. I'm looking for somewhere to live.
A: OK, well, you've come to the right place ... just give me a second ... Right, the first thing we need to do is complete an accommodation form, OK?
C: OK.
A: Could you tell me your surname please.
C: Yes, it's Minguez.
A: OK, is that M-I-N-G-E-Z?
C: No, it's M-I-N-G-U-E-Z
A: OK, thank you. And your first name?
C: It's Carlos-Jerez
A: Hmm, so that's initials C. J.
C: Yes.
A: And are you married, Carlos?
C: No, I'm not.
A: OK. What do you do for a living, Carlos?
C: Sorry, I don't understand.
A: What's your job?
C: Oh, I don't have a job. I'm studying at university at the moment.
A: OK, no problem. And what kind of accommodation are you looking for, Carlos?
C: Um, I'm looking for a house with three bedrooms for me and my two friends.
A: OK, so that's three singles. Do you want to live on the outskirts of town?
C: No, we'd like to live in the centre. We haven't got cars and we need to get to the shops and the university.

Recording 02

1 /eɪ/ J, K, A, H,
2 /iː/ C, D, E, T, B, G, P, V
3 /e/ M, N, X, F, L, S, Z
4 /aɪ/ I, Y
5 /əʊ/ O
6 /uː/ U, W, Q

Recording 03

1 1 zero, double seven, triple eight, nine, seven, six, three, six, four
  2 zero, seven, triple eight, nine, seven, six, three, six, four
  3 zero, triple seven, double eight, nine, seven, six, three, six, four
2 1 four hundred and two pounds
  2 forty-two pounds
  3 four thousand and two pounds
3 1 the eighteenth of September, two thousand and thirteen
  2 the tenth of August, two thousand and thirteen
  3 the eighth of September, two thousand and thirteen

4 1 h, underscore, Atkinson, at, twinky, dot, i, t
  2 h, a, at, atkins, underscore, i, t
  3 h, dot, atkins, hyphen, son, at, twinky, dot, i, t

Recording 04

[A= Accommodation officer, C = Carlos]
A: Hmm. That's going to be more expensive you know. How much can you spend?
C: No more than £100.
A: Per week?
C: No, per month.
A: I'm sorry Carlos, you won't find anything for that price around here.
C: OK, well our maximum is £300 per month, but that must include bills.
A: OK, I'll see what I can do. It won't be easy though. Would you like to rent the house for a year?
C: No. If possible, we'd like to rent it until July. From then we're going to be studying abroad.
A: Lucky you! So, you'll only need the house for nine months?
C: That's right.
A: Well, we're in September now, so if you want the house for nine months, your rent will be starting in October.
C: Yes, my friends arrive in England from Spain on October 15th.
A: Hmm. That's not long, but I'll do my best to find you something.
C: Thank you very much.
A: No problem, I'll be in touch ... Oh, nearly forgot. Do you have a phone number?
C: Yes, but only a mobile, it's 0778 8976364
A: So that's 0778 88976364?
C: No, 07788...976364
A: Got it. And your email?
C: Um, it's c.minguez@granadino.es, so that's c, dot, M-I-N-G-U-E-Z, at, G-R-A-N-A-D-I-N-O, dot, E-S.
A: Right. See you soon.
C: See you, bye.

Recording 05

[A= Aisha, L = Linda]
A: Morning Linda!
L: Morning Aisha, how's my favourite flat mate?
A: Your only flat mate you mean! I'm OK but I'm getting a bit stressed about student clubs.
L: Why? They're supposed to be fun. It's studying that's the hard part.
A: Yes, I know, but the problem is that I don't know which club to join and they all need us to enrol now – in the first week of term.
L: Well, which club do you want to join? I've thought about the basketball club, but I'm not sure if I can go to all of the practice sessions. One of them, on Wednesday evening, is at the same time as an evening lab lesson I have.
A: Yes, well that is a problem because one of the rules is that your attendance must be 75%. I suppose if you don't go to most of the sessions, it's a waste of money.

L: 75%! That's a lot. Still, it's probably worth it; you must meet a lot of interesting people. What club were you thinking about joining?

A: I was actually thinking about joining a couple – you get a 20% discount if you join more than one. One of the clubs I think I'd like to join is Aikido.

L: Isn't that the one where people hit each other with long sticks?

A: Well … sort of.

L: I don't know. It sounds like it could be dangerous and it must be difficult to make friends if you're hitting them.

L: How about rowing?

A: Mmm. I'm not sure about the rowing club. I mean, I like exercise but I've heard that the rowers get up at six every day. I sometimes can't get motivated to get out of bed for lectures that start at 9!

L: Good point. I personally like clubs which allow me to relax a bit and have a bit of fun.

A: Yeah, me too. I think choir sounds like it could be exciting; I'm definitely thinking about joining that.

L: Really? I don't think I can sing and anyway, are you sure it would be that much fun?

A: Well, how about this …

L: Ballroom dancing?! You MUST be joking!

A: Oh, come on Linda, it would be fun and anyway, it would make you light on your feet – a great skill for a basketball player to have.

L: OK, you've convinced me. But I'm only going to enrol for this term. That way, if I hate it, we can change – we'll go rowing instead.

Recording 06

[TO= Tourist officer, Tu = Tutor]

TO: 'Czech Tours', can I help you?

Tu: Oh, yes, hello, I hope so. I'd like to bring a group of music and drama students to Prague in a few months' time and I need some help organizing some trips for them.

TO: OK, I'll try to help you. But I need to take some details about the group first, OK?

Tu: Yes, that's fine.

TO: Right, first of all, how many people are there in your group?

Tu: Well, I've still got to confirm numbers. Not everyone is sure that they can come. But I think there will be about 15, not including me and another tutor.

TO: OK, and how old are they?

Tu: Oh, they're all adults; they're second year undergraduates, so between nineteen and twenty years old.

TO: That's fine for now, but I'll need exact ages and names if you decide to book with us, OK?
OK. So, when would you like to visit Prague?

Tu: Um, we think it'll be the second week in September for a week … uh, let me look at a calendar.

TO: So, that's the fifth of September to the eleventh?

Tu: The fifth is a Monday isn't it? Um, no, I think we want to fly at the weekend so that we have the full week in Prague. We'll try to book plane tickets on Saturday the 3rd and travel back on the following Saturday.

TO: The tenth of September?

Tu: That's right. So we'll need accommodation for seven nights. We're hoping to stay in a youth hostel, to keep costs as low as possible.

TO: That shouldn't be a problem, but I don't organize accommodation myself, only activities. I can give you some useful numbers though.

Tu: Yes please.

TO: Right, well, you could try Charles Bridge Hostel; it's right near the centre and it's quite reasonable, about 690 koruna or 30 euros per person per night. If you don't have any luck with that, you could try the Castle Hostel. It's not as central and it's at the top of a very steep hill, but it's very nice.

Tu: It's good to have a second option. How much is that?

TO: It's actually a bit cheaper, 25 euros a night, so that's about the same in pounds sterling.

Tu: OK, can I have the numbers of both hostels?

TO: Charles Bridge Hostel is on 486 899 666.

Tu: Great, that's 486 899 666.

TO: Yes and don't forget to dial 00 420 from England before the number.

Tu: OK.

TO: It's probably better to send the Castle Hostel an email. It's castlehostel@prahaworld.ch, that's C-A-S-T-L-E-H-O-S-T-E-L, AT, P-R-A-H-A-W-O-R-L-D, dot, C-H.

Tu: Great. Thank you, I'll try the Charles Bridge Hostel now.

TO: That's fine, but there's no rush. They're open from 9 until late. You can ring up to midnight.

Recording 07

Good afternoon. I'm Theo Onassis, your social services officer. I'm here to make your time in England as easy as possible. I've had over eight years' experience of working with students who come here to study from other countries and I was once a student myself. I have to warn you that, although there will be wonderful moments in your time here, you will also have times when all you want to do is to go home. You can deal with these times by understanding that this is a process that you, and every other student is going through. It's called 'culture shock' and I'm going to explain the different stages to you.

The first phase is the most positive. That's why a lot of people call it the 'honeymoon phase'. You've just come to England, everything is new and exciting and you are looking forward to having lots of new experiences. Typically this phase lasts about two weeks, but it can last for a couple of months.

It may be that after a few months your feelings change. This is the second phase of the process, 'culture shock'. It could be that something bad happens. For example, you might meet an English person who isn't as helpful as you hope. When this happens, a lot of foreign students feel angry or frustrated and they stay with other people from their country because it seems safer. Try not to do this; it will only make you feel lonely and less at home in the long run.

The third phase of culture shock is learning how to live with it, or 'coping'. There are a number of things you can do to make you feel better. One student I know offered to teach an English person about her language and culture. The English person learned some Arabic and the student's English improved a lot. They are now good friends. Another thing you can do is to cook your favourite dishes using ingredients you buy locally, and then invite all your new friends round. Most importantly, try not to sit at home all day feeling down. Get out there and find all the things you *do* like about living here.

When a student has stopped suffering from culture shock, they begin to accept the way of life here in England and get used to staying here. This doesn't mean that you understand everything about England but that you know what makes you happy here. This is the final stage of the culture shock process. Of course, by the time you do this, your three years of study here will probably be over and it'll be time to go home!

Recording 08

1 staff
2 Audiology
3 North
4 Clinical
5 Reception

Recording 09

Good morning and welcome to your first day of your student placement at our wonderful hospital. I do hope that your time spent here will be interesting.

Right, well, as you'll already have seen, the hospital site is enormous, and it's quite easy to get lost, so I'll start by showing you a map. At the moment, you are situated here, just in front of the reception in the main entrance. To the north of here are the staff apartments, where you'll be staying while you work here. If you go through the double doors here to the right of reception, and head east along the corridor here, you come to the Accident and Emergency ward or A&E for short.

Recording 10

[continues from 09]

If you continue to go east, you come to the Audiology Clinic, for patients with bad hearing; you'll be spending about a week of your placement here.

To the south of the Audiology Clinic, across the road, you'll find eight bus stops. You can take a bus into town from here, along Keith Day Road, if you have some spare time. So, to continue, behind the bus stops, on the right of the map is the Clinical School, where you will have most of your lessons when you're not visiting patients with our doctors. Between this and the Rosie Hospital at the other end of the site are the wards, where most of the patients sleep. You'll see that the wards are named with letters of the alphabet. Ward A is next to Ward B and to the left of that is Ward C etc. Between Wards D and E is a set of lifts – these small squares here – which will take you up to the second floor and wards M–Z.

Right, now I'll take you to have a look at your apartments. Before I do, can I ask if any of you have cars? Yes? If so, you can leave your car in the staff car park, to the west of reception. I hope that's all clear. Has anyone got any questions?

Recording 11

Good afternoon everyone. Thank you very much for volunteering on our new student mentor programme. Now, the first year students will begin to arrive in two weeks' time and we need to be ready for them. Our first task is to be at halls of residence to welcome them and show them to their rooms. You'll each have about twenty students to meet and greet, so you'll be very busy.

Once the students have seen where they'll be staying, they'll need to visit the rest of the campus. Your second task is to show small groups of students the main facilities like the library, the doctors and the Central Hall. Please don't worry about explaining how everything works in detail to students; it's best to keep it simple on their first day.

When the tour is finished, please bring your students to the Central Hall. Here, they'll sign some important forms and pick up their student card, which will allow them in and out of all the buildings. As you know, security is quite high.

After that, you need to take them to the college canteens for an evening meal. The rest of the evening is yours to do what you want with, but you might like to stay with the new students who could be feeling a bit lost.

OK, now, with 1,000 new students out and about on the same day, we need to make sure that everyone knows where they're going and when. Here's a map showing the tour route we'd like you to take around the university campus. I'd like everyone to meet here at midday, at the Central Hall. We're then going to split into four groups and one group will leave the hall every ten minutes, so that the campus doesn't get too crowded.

When you leave the hall, please go through the main entrance and cross the bridge across the lake. Have a quick look around the Central Library and then go north-east, towards the Science Block. If you have any science students, show them the laboratories and then turn right and go south towards the students' centre. While you're there, it's probably a good idea to show them where the bus stops are across the road so that they can catch the bus into town.

Then, to end the tour, head behind the Central Hall towards the Halls of Residence. It's a good idea to show them the computer rooms and leisure centre to the north of there.

Recording 12

[S = Sue, DL = Dr Lillie]

S: Oh, hello Dr Lillie. Thanks very much for agreeing to see me.

DL: No problem at all Sue. You sounded a little worried on the phone. How can I help?

S: It's this end of year essay. You said that we can write about one of the nine topics we've studied this term, but I don't know which one to choose.

DL: Oh yes, I remember. Well, I hoped that you would write about the topic that interested you the most.

S: But the trouble is, I've enjoyed everything we've studied this year. I found the module on Victorian photography fascinating, and the seminar on 19th-century art really made me think about what the word 'modern' means…

DL: Well, I'm very glad you feel so enthusiastic. Let's look at this in another way. Can you remember which subjects you got the best marks for?

S: Hmm. Well, I didn't do very well on the photography course; I only got 60% for my essay. I think you said I needed to look more at how photography influenced painting.

DL: That's right, I think I did … but you did very well in the assignment on modern art didn't you – 90%! And your seminar presentation was also excellent.

S: Thank you! Though I'm not sure I have much more to say about art in the late 19th and 20th century.

DL: But there are hundreds of books on modern art and lots you could write about, perhaps you should look into it a bit further?

Recording 13

[S = Sue, DL = Dr Lillie]

S: I'm sure you're right, but I'm having trouble thinking of ideas. If you remember, I wrote about how industry changed the art of impressionist painters, like Claude Monet. I'd prefer not to write about the same paintings again.

DL: Yes, I agree you need another angle. Let's see … have you thought about the role that women artists played in modern art?

S: I could try that I suppose, but it does sound quite difficult ... I can't think of many 19th-century female artists. Um, let's see ... there's Berthe Morisot, Mary Cassatt ... I can only think of two.

DL: Well, that's because women of that time didn't really have a role in public life. They stayed at home and looked after the family.

S: So that's why artists like Morisot painted rooms in her house and her children, not scenes from the outside world.

DL: Exactly.

S: Well, I might write about that, but I'm not sure it inspires me ...

DL: Well, if you're not sure about that, you may like to consider more contemporary artists.

S: I haven't really studied contemporary art yet ... but I did read an article recently about an artist called Karla Black who used makeup like lipstick and nail varnish in her art.

DL: Well, there are lots of 21st century artists who use unusual materials to make art. Look at Marc Quinn who used his own blood to make a sculpture of his head, or Chris Offili who used elephant dung!

S: Gosh! ... that's really interesting – I'd like to know more about why they chose to do that. I'll definitely research that further.

Recording 14
[C = Claire, J = Josh, T = Tutor]

T: So, now that you've completed one term at your schools, we need to look at the subject of your first assignment. I think that each of you should focus on an area which you had difficulties with at your schools. So, Claire, tell me about your experience.

C: Well, at first I thought that I'd have trouble with the students, but actually, they were all really easy to deal with.

T: That's good. I should warn you though that you might find teaching teenagers more difficult.

C: OK. I hope not though. The thing I did have problems with was my work–life balance. I found that I had no time at all after preparing lessons and marking homework to relax. This worries me a bit.

T: Did this affect how you were in the classroom?

C: Yes, I think so. I was less patient with some of the students. Also, I don't think I could work that hard for long periods of time without a rest – I think I'd go mad!

T: Well, yes, teaching is demanding, but it's important to find a balance. I'd suggest then, you read some books that give advice about managing time; you might find some useful tips in the business books in the library.

C: OK, thank you.

T: And what about you Josh? I've had some positive feedback from your school.

J: Yes, I've enjoyed this term a lot. Like Claire, I really like the students and I think they feel the same.

T: Well, a good relationship is very important. But do you think that the students are actually learning anything?

J: Yes and no. The trouble I have is that I think I talk too much.

T: I can't believe that, Josh!

J: Yes, well ... I want to tell them everything I know, but they just seem to lose interest after a while.

T: Well, don't you remember how difficult it is to concentrate on lectures at university? Have you tried to get students to find things out for themselves? Perhaps you could get them to do some project work, so that they take responsibility for their own learning?

J: That's a good idea.

T: I suggest looking at references on independent study and guided learning. I can lend you a couple of books if you like.

Recording 15
[C = Claire, J = Josh, T = Tutor]

T: So let's talk about what's happening next term. Josh, we're suggesting you move to Summer High for a term.

J: Oh, that's a shame. I've really enjoyed teaching the classes at Elm Grove.

T: Yes, well, I know you've built relationships with students at this school but we think you need experience of an inner-city school, with children with a wider range of backgrounds.

J: But I'm making some progress with the kids at this school.

T: Try to remember this is just training. There will be time to build lasting relationships when you get your first permanent teaching job. Sorry Josh, my decision is final on this one. Claire, how do you feel about teaching year 10s next year?

C: Hmm. It depends on which set.

T: Well, you've taught the top set of students in Year 11.

C: Yeah, they were great; such an intelligent group of students. I hardly had to encourage them at all.

T: Exactly. I think now you need to teach people who find learning difficult in some cases.

C: OK, well, it'll certainly be a challenge. I'm a bit worried about one of the students though; he can be a trouble-maker.

T: Make sure you tell a senior member of staff if you get into real difficulties.

C: OK

T: Well, I'm very pleased with how you've done so far, and I really think that next term will give you some valuable experience. I'm sure you'll do very well.

Recording 16

1 Good morning, everyone, and thank you all for coming to my talk. As you may know, as part of our training to become dieticians, we have to do some research into an aspect of dietary health. You've already heard talks from my classmates on diabetes and eating problems or 'eating disorders' among teenage girls who are influenced by images in magazines.

2 My research falls into two parts. The first part consisted of primary research; I collected data by conducting a survey. About a fifth of the people questioned were women with young children. They said that they had gained weight during pregnancy and then couldn't lose it again.

3 About one in ten people questioned weren't worried about their weight at all. These tended to be people over the age of 70. Interestingly, these people were aware that sugary, fatty food could lead to weight problems.

4 Around a quarter of people interviewed worked ten to twelve hours a day or more and typically, spent a lot of time sitting in front of a computer. This group generally said that they ate healthily but didn't exercise enough to burn the calories off.

5 Just over 30% of people thought they overate because of how they felt. This group tended to be women in their twenties.

Recording 17

Good morning, everyone, and thank you all for coming to my talk. As you may know, as part of our training to become dieticians, we have to do some research into an aspect of dietary health. You've already heard talks from my classmates on diabetes and eating problems or 'eating disorders' among teenage girls who are influenced by images in magazines. I've chosen to focus instead on people who eat too much and become overweight. Being medically overweight or, 'obese', is a growing problem worldwide and I wanted to investigate the reasons behind this issue.

My research falls into two parts. The first part consisted of primary research; I collected data by conducting a survey. About a fifth of the people questioned were women with young children. They said that they had gained weight during pregnancy and then couldn't lose it again. They thought that they put on weight because of a bad diet; they spent all their time looking after their children and not enough time thinking about their choice of food.

About one in ten people questioned weren't worried about their weight at all. These tended to be people over the age of 70. Interestingly, these people were aware that sugary, fatty food could lead to weight problems but chose an unhealthy diet because it gave them, they thought, a better quality of life.

Around a quarter of people interviewed worked ten to twelve hours or more and typically, spent a lot of time sitting in front of a computer. This group generally said that they ate healthily but didn't exercise enough to burn the calories off. After a long day in the office, they felt too tired to work out at the gym.

Just over 30% of people thought they overate because of how they felt. This group tended to be women in their twenties. They said that their weight went up and down, depending on whether they were going through a good or difficult period of their lives.

Recording 18

Now to come onto the second part of my research. This focused on global obesity. Obesity is measured using the BMI or the Body Mass Index. This is used to calculate your ideal weight on the basis of how tall you are. Using this measurement, researchers have found that levels of obesity are at 5% in China and Japan. In contrast, in England, Germany, and the USA, up to 75% of the population are obese. Levels of obesity in children are worrying; it's estimated that world-wide, in 79 developing countries, over 22 million children under the age of five are overweight. But why is obesity a growing problem? Well, researchers have found a number of explanations. Firstly, there is a relationship between age and weight; when people reach the age of 50, they tend to put on weight. There's also a link between weight and location. People living in the countryside tend to have active lives so it's more difficult to put on weight than if you live in the city. Unfortunately, more people in developing countries are moving into cities to live and work.

Recording 19

Hi, everyone. Thanks for coming. Well, it's certainly an exciting time to be studying palaeontology at the moment. As many of you may have heard on the news, there has been a discovery in Kazakhstan which questions our beliefs about what lived on the earth 100 million years ago. Two bones which have been discovered in the desert belong to a huge bird, named *Samrukia nessovi* that lived at the same time as dinosaurs.

Up to now, palaeontologists thought that dinosaurs and large birds did not live at the same time. Research suggested dinosaurs lived on the earth first, died, and then large birds came along quite a long time after that. Until now, palaeontologists thought that birds living alongside dinosaurs were only the size of chickens.

So, how big was the bird? Well, the bones discovered are 27cm long and are part of the bird's jaw, which means that its head was probably about 30cm long. It's likely, then, that the bird was at least three metres tall, and over 50kg in weight. If the bird lived today, it would be bigger than an ostrich.

This doesn't, of course, make it the biggest bird ever to have lived on earth. The elephant bird of Madagascar, which was related to the ostrich, was much heavier, at around 500kg. The giant moa of New Zealand was taller at nearly four metres. But neither of these birds are as old as the one found in Kazakhstan.

There are many questions surrounding the recent discovery. The most significant one is, of course, could it fly? Unfortunately, as only the jaw bones have been discovered, it's impossible to answer that question. We just hope that more discoveries take place. If it did fly, the width of its wings was probably over four metres.

I haven't mentioned yet that this isn't the first discovery of this kind. Another large bird, named *Gargantuavis*, that lived in southern France 70 million years ago, was discovered in the late 1990s. The discovery of *Samrukia nessovi* proves unquestionably that large birds and dinosaurs lived side by side.

Recording 20

Good afternoon, everybody. Thanks for attending this talk. As many of you may already be aware, a career in fashion design is very exciting. But, you may also know that fashion design doesn't always pay the bills. To make more money, it may be necessary for you to move into a slightly different area of the business. I'm here to talk to you about the area of fashion marketing. In particular, I'd like to give you an idea of what fashion marketing is. I'll also describe the types of jobs a fashion marketer does. I'll end by talking about challenges in the job and give you some suggestions about how you can become a successful fashion marketer.

So, to start with, a definition of marketing. Marketing involves thinking about what the customer wants and needs. When a customer, or consumer buys a piece of clothing, a pair of shoes for example, they might think about how long the product will last. This is called its durability. Or the customer might think about the style of the shoes, whether they are fashionable. Of course, the consumer will also need the shoes to be comfortable. Fashion marketers need to remember that there are different types of consumer; some may spend £200 on a pair of designer shoes and some may spend £50. Marketers need to consider who the typical consumer is for a product and whether this consumer belongs to a bigger group of people who would buy the product. This group is the product's key market.

As you are all consumers, you'll all be aware of advertising. But this is just one of the areas that fashion marketers work in. They also work in product development, branding, pricing, publicity, sales promotion, selling and forecasting.

The area of fashion marketing you choose to work in will depend on your interests and skills. If you enjoy meeting members of the public, market research may be for you. You will conduct surveys, watch how your competitors are doing and whether they have a bigger share of the market than your company has. Another exciting role is marketing manager. Imagine you want to sell a shirt to a particular chain of stores. You have to make sure that the shirt goes with other items of clothing that the store sells. You also need to think about the type of consumer that shops at the store and you need to convince the store to buy the shirt.

You may be thinking, 'but I'm a fashion designer. I'm creative and I'm not interested in business at all.' You may see fashion marketing as rather boring. I've been working in this industry for twenty years and it's definitely not boring. Fashion marketers have a huge amount of power. After all, we choose what thousands of people around the world wear. If you decide to train as a fashion marketer though, you will need to prepare yourself for hard work and tight deadlines. Lots of people will have more experience than you and you may not be able to find jobs working with clothes in the first few years. My advice to you is to get some unpaid work experience while you are training. This will make you more attractive for future employers.

I hope that gives you an idea of Fashion Marketing. If you think that you might be interested in working in this area, please come and collect one of my business cards. I'd be very interested in receiving your CVs …

Speaking module

Recording 21
[E = Examiner, CA = Candidate A, CB = Candidate B]

Candidate A
E: Tell me a bit about your job.
CA: Well, um, it's an interested job. I work in a school. The other teachers and I work very long hours. We are getting very tired at the end of um, er, the … I don't know the word … oh yes … term. The students are good. In general, I like it.

Candidate B
E: Tell me a bit about your job.
CB: Well, I don't have a paid job, but I do work very hard every day. Um, I'm a … I'm a mother and I look after my children at home. My children are two and four years old and I gave up my job when my eldest was one. It was too much, you know, working full-time and then rushing home to see them. And anyway, it made me feel bad. I'm much happier now. Usually the start of the day is busy because my children need to eat breakfast and get dressed and my husband is trying to get to work. The rest of the day is more relaxed though.

Recording 22
There are lots of places I like but one of my favourite places is in Croatia. It's a city called Dubrovnik. I first visited Dubrovnik when I was very little, so I don't remember that much. I remember that I went with my family and it was my first holiday abroad. I've since been back to Dubrovnik lots of times. Last year I went with my husband and we had a lovely time, as usual. What I like about Dubrovnik is its location. It's right next to the sea. You can stand on the old city walls and look out over miles of blue ocean. The good thing about this is that you can combine a city break with lots of swimming and sunbathing. My husband likes art so we sometimes go to art galleries in the city in the mornings. During the afternoons, we take a boat out to one of the little islands nearby. It's perfect.

Recording 23
One of my favourite art works is called *David* and it's a sculpture. It's made from Italian marble, taken from the mountains near Carrara, in Tuscany. It's a very big sculpture; about five metres tall.

The place where I first saw *David* was in a big square in Florence, called Piazza di Signoria. I learnt later that this is only a copy of the original statue. The original is in the Academia gallery in Florence.

An artist called Michelangelo created the sculpture. He lived and worked in the 15th century. He's a very famous artist. He made lots of amazing sculptures and he painted the Sistine Chapel in Rome, too.

The reason I like the statue is that it says something interesting. It shows a young man who has killed the bad giant Goliath. This means that it's possible for a good person to beat a bad person, even if the evil person is stronger.

Recording 24
Example A
The person I admire the most is my mother. The reason I think she's wonderful is that she has always put her children first. When we were young, she didn't have much money at all, but we were never hungry and she even managed to take us on holiday. She's now an old lady but she still tries to look after me. She always tries to give me food when I visit her.

Example B
(as above)

Recording 25
[CA = Candidate A, CB = Candidate B, CC = Candidate C, E = Examiner]

Candidate A
CA: This is a difficult question to answer because I've always had the Internet, so I can't imagine life without it.
E: Yes, I see what you mean.
CA: But, um, in my opinion, the Internet has many advantages. For example, it brings people together. It's possible to talk to someone living on the other side of the world with an internet program. It also saves a great deal of time. Before, if a person wanted some information, it was necessary to go to the library, whereas now, you can just look it up online in five minutes. Unfortunately, there are some disadvantages, like people can find information about you online and use it to steal your identity or even take money from your bank account. Overall, though, I think there are more advantages than disadvantages.

Candidate B

CB: I believe that it's much more important to have good friends than to be rich. Um, I don't think that money can buy you happiness. There are examples of people who have won the lottery and then given the money away because it didn't improve their lives. It seems that money can actually make you lonely. Perhaps people want to be your friend just because you have money, not because they are interested in you. Real friends, on the other hand, stay with you whether you are rich or poor and help you through the hard times. It's much better to have good friends than money.

E: Those are all interesting points, but what if someone doesn't have any money at all? Won't that cause unhappiness?

CB: Yes, I agree with you. Money is important to live, but I don't think you need lots of it.

Candidate C

CC: Well, I hope that we will have more spare time in the future. This should be the case because we have a lot of time saving machines now that we didn't have in the past. For instance, my grandmother used to spend a whole day each week doing the washing by hand ...

E: Really? That long?

CC: Yes, absolutely. But fortunately, nowadays, we can just put the washing in a machine and go off and have some fun. In the future, scientists will probably invent more time-saving machines which will mean less work for us. However, I'm afraid that we won't have more spare time because these days, everything happens more quickly so people expect work to be done in a shorter time. This puts people under a lot of pressure, and means that sometimes, um, people work longer hours and actually have less free time. Realistically, I think that it's unlikely that people will have more free time in the future.

Practice test

Recording 26

[Ma = Magda, Mo = Mohammed]

Ma: Hello.

Mo: Oh, hello, can I speak to Magda please?

Ma: Yes, this is Magda here.

Mo: Hi, Magda, my name's Mohammed. I'm phoning about the car advertised on the college notice board. Is it still available?

Ma: Yes, it is. A few people have come to see it, but they all want newer, faster cars.

Mo: That was my first question actually. How old is the car?

Ma: It's nine years old ... but it doesn't look it.

Mo: Mmm, that's good. And how many miles has it done?

Ma: Well the mileometer says 40,000.

Mo: That seems quite low for a car of that age. I think maybe the mileometer is broken!

Ma: No, I think it's because the previous owner was an old lady and she didn't use it that much.

Mo: Right, great. Can I ask why you're selling the car?

Ma: Yes, sure. I've just got a job in London. I can take the tube so I don't need a car.

Mo: That's great, congratulations. Um, could I just check the price? Uh, the advert says £600 which seems quite a lot for an old car.

Ma: Not really, when you think it hasn't done many miles. I can take £100 off the final price, but that's it I'm afraid.

Mo: OK, that seems fair. Could I come and see the car this evening?

Ma: Um, well, tonight's not great, but I could manage tomorrow.

Mo: Fine. Shall we say around 11am?

Ma: OK. Shall I drive the car to you?

Mo: That's really kind, thanks. I live on campus: we could meet in the café; I'll buy you a coffee to say thanks.

Ma: Sure, I'll be there around half past eleven.

Mo: Great, see you there.

Recording 27

[I = Insurance broker, Mo = Mohammed]

I: Good afternoon, Wayne's Wheels, can I help you?

Mo: Um, hello, yes, I've just bought a car and I need some insurance.

I: OK, I'll ask you some questions and see what we can do to help.

Mo: All right.

I: So, let's start with your full name.

Mo: My name is Mohammed Al-Shariff.

I: I'm sorry, can you spell your surname?

Mo: Yes, it's A-L, hyphen, S-H-A-R-I-F-F.

I: Thanks, and when were you born Mohammed?

Mo: I was born on the 21st of October 1994.

I: So you're 19. Great. And what sort of car have you bought?

Mo: It's a Peugeot 205 Diesel.

I: Mmm. Have you got the registration number?

Mo: Yes, it's YL34 GGB.

I: OK, can I have your address?

Mo: Yes, it's 78 Acacia Avenue, Stourbridge, Wolverhampton, BM56 YLM.

I: Is that A-C-A-C-I-A?

Mo: That's right.

I: Well, the good news is that the computer is saying that Stourbridge is a safe area, so this will keep the price of your insurance down.

Mo: That's good. Do you know how much it'll be?

I: Well ... the system is quoting me a price of £100.

Mo: Per year?

I: No, per month, I'm afraid and you'll need to pay an extra £50 in the first month which is the administration charge.

Mo: OK, so that's £1,250 in total for the year?

I: That's right. Now, how would you like to pay? ...

Recording 28

Hi there, everybody. Thank you so much for coming. In the room here today we have students from Japan, Afghanistan, Europe and North America. Some of you have English as your first language but the majority don't. You all have something in common though; everyone here works in the field of law, and you are all here for our new blended learning course, which allows you to get the qualification you need without leaving your country or your job.

So, this two-day conference is one of only two chances that you will get to meet your tutors and your classmates face-to-face in your first year of study. The next time we meet it'll be for a lot longer; our three-month summer intensive course, which ends with your end-of-year exams.

You'll be doing all of your online learning on our Virtual Learning Platform, or VLP for short. This is a set of online tools which help you to study and allow your work to be assessed.

So, how will you use the VLP? Well, first of all, when you return to your country, you need to log on to the VLP and then download your first assignment and the reading list.

Then you will need to find the books on the reading list. Some of the books will be available to download from the VLP, but you may have to buy some on the Internet.

While you are studying for your first assignment, if you have any questions, please feel free to write your tutor an email. If you'd prefer, you can arrange to have a phone conversation with your tutor instead.

If you've asked your tutor for help and you don't want to contact them again, you can try the student forum. There will be lots of other students who will be happy to help. After you've submitted your first assignment, you can expect to wait about a week before your tutor uploads your grade onto the VLP.

Assignments are a fairly small part of the course, however. A lot more time will be spent participating in seminars and listening to lectures. There is one seminar per week, which you'll be able to participate in on the VLP. We try to choose a convenient time for everyone but you may find that your seminar is very early in the morning or late at night. There are also five lectures per week. These are recorded and uploaded onto the VLP and you can listen to them at a convenient time.

Now, I think you all know that balancing a full-time job with studying isn't easy. It may be that, from time to time, you can't meet a deadline. If this happens, let your tutor know and they will discuss how much extra time you need. There's also the option, in the most serious cases, to extend your degree, to give you another year of study time. We don't encourage you to do this. However, it is an option and we can discuss it with you if necessary.

So, that brings me to the end of my talk. Has anybody got any questions? I know it's a lot to take in ...

Recording 29

{T = Tutor, J = Jane}
T: Morning, Jane, thanks for coming to see me, take a seat.
J: Thank you, Dr Coulson.
T: Now, you're probably wondering why I wanted to talk to you.
J: Well, yes, it has been worrying me a bit.
T: No need to worry. I just wanted to have a chat about your progress this term and in particular, discuss your research project.
J: OK.
T: So, I should start by saying that you're a very active member of the seminar group. You have always prepared well for the seminars by reading around the subject, which is good.
J: Thank you. I find the seminars very interesting. I try to listen to the group's ideas as well.
T: Yes, you **are** very good at listening, but I feel that you accept the ideas suggested in the group a little too easily.
J: I'm sorry, I'm not sure what you mean.
T: Well, do you remember the lecture on critical thinking I gave?
J: Um, yes, I think so. It was all about asking questions.
T: Well, that's partly right, but it's the type of questions you ask that is important. For example, if one of the people in your group expresses an idea, you need to ask yourself what evidence there is to support this idea.
J: OK, I'll try to do that. You mentioned my research project as well?

T: Yes, it's actually connected to the idea of critical thinking. I'm a little concerned that the essay makes some statements which I'm not sure your research completely proves. For example, you make the claim that people who have difficulty with their speech probably had an accident when they were young.
J: Yes, that's because my case study had a very bad car accident as a child and since then he has not been able to speak properly.
T: OK, that's interesting. But I think you need a greater quantity of data to support your findings. You can't really rely on case studies alone. They're a great source of in-depth information about individuals, but they don't really provide us with the quantity of information needed to make general claims. Have you checked whether there are any research papers which talk about the connection between accidents and speech?
J: Not yet, no, but I will.
T: Yes, do. They might analyze what happens in the brain after an accident and why this might affect speech. Remember to check the date the article was written though; research tends to go out of date quickly. Have you also interviewed experts who argue against the connection between speech problems and accidents?
J: No, I thought that that would weaken my argument.
T: Well, it may well do. But it doesn't really matter what you believe in the end, you just need to think about the evidence on both sides and make a reasoned judgement.
J: OK, I think I see what you mean. I was also thinking about getting a higher quantity of information through sending this questionnaire out to medical institutions. Would you mind having a look at it for me ...
T: Yes, sure, let's see ... Well, on the whole, it's fine, I think. But you need to be very careful about asking 'leading questions'. What I mean by that is some of your questions may actually suggest what answer you are looking for.
J: That's helpful. Thank you. I'll change those questions.
T: Good. So, when do you think you'll have a first draft for me to look at?

Recording 30

Hello everybody. So, as part of our study programme this term, we've researched an aspect of archaeology which has some kind of mystery attached to it. I'm going to talk about the mysteries of the Great Pyramids of Egypt. In particular, I'm going to concentrate on the theories surrounding how the pyramids were built. I'm going to start by putting pyramids into their historical context. Then I'm going to look at the different ideas surrounding the building of the pyramids. At the end there will be the chance to ask questions.

So, why are we so fascinated with the building of the pyramids? Well it's to do with their enormous size and weight. The Great Pyramid of Khufu, for example, at Giza in Egypt, has a mass of 5.9 million tons and it is around 146 metres tall. Approximately 2.3 million stone blocks were used to build it. Today's architects would have difficulties building a pyramid of this size and weight in the middle of a desert, even with the help of powered machinery. For the architects of 2550 BC, who didn't have modern technology to help them, building a pyramid must have been almost impossible. There's no doubt that they had a big work force. During the 80 years of building this pyramid, between 20,000 and 30,000 workers helped with its construction. However, this doesn't explain how workers could lift and move a stone block which weighed over two tons. There have been several theories about this from leading archaeologists.

One common theory states that a straight ramp, or slope, was built outside the pyramid and workers could walk up the ramp, pulling the stone block. This diagram, at the top, illustrates the theory. As you can see, one problem is the size of the ramp. In order to get it to reach right to the top of the pyramid, the ramp would have to be around 1 km long. There wasn't the space for this sort of ramp; pyramids were built on a high platform, with other buildings around them, as shown in the diagram.

This second diagram shows another theory, which has been suggested by French architect Jean-Pierre Houdin. Houdin believes that a shorter, 60-metre long ramp was used on the outside of the pyramid. Workers would pull the stone blocks up the ramp in order to build the base of the pyramid. As the bottom of the pyramid was being built using the external ramp, a second ramp was being built, inside the pyramid. The internal ramp begins at the bottom, is about 6 feet wide, and is much less steep than a large, external straight ramp would be.

So, I've outlined two of the main theories associated with the building of the pyramids. I personally think that Houdin's theory is the most believable. However, I'd like to know your opinions. Would anyone like to say what they think or ask a question? …. [